# THE
# ❧ CASTLES OF WALES ❧

*Caernarfon Castle*

*John Idris Jones*

# THE
# CASTLES
## OF
# WALES

## Alan Reid

JOHN JONES

The Castles of Wales
text copyright © Alan Reid 1998
typography & lay-out copyright © John Jones Publishing Ltd 1998

First published in paperback March 1998
New edition May 1999

ISBN 1 871083 41 9

*Frontispiece: Caernarfon Castle. Photograph by John Idris Jones.
All other photographs used in this book are Crown Copyright,
and are reproduced by permission of the
Controller of Her Majesty's Stationery Office.*

Printed and bound in Great Britain by
Dinefwr Press, Llandybie, Carmarthenshire, Wales

Published by John Jones Publishing Ltd,
Unit 12, Clwydfro Centre, Ruthin, North Wales LL15 1NJ

## CASTLE BUILDING IN BRITAIN

T HE dictionary defines a castle as any stronghold or fortified group of buildings; however, many purists, for example D. O'Neil who wrote the introductory guide to *"Castles of England and Wales"* published in 1954 by H.M.S.O., limit their definition to those strongholds erected since the Norman Conquest. The word itself is derived from *castella* which is the diminutive form of *castrum*, Latin for a fort, so that there is no etymological reason for such a limiting definition.

The legions of Rome never camped at night without erecting some form of defensive works, and in the barrack towns these were made elaborate and permanent. When the Romans left these shores in the 5th Century A.D. the Saxon *burgh* or *tun* became the conventional form of defence, whereby the town or village was surrounded by some fortification such as a ditch or a wall of timber. The difference between these burghs and the castles of the Middle Ages was that the first were essentially public defences while those constructed from the Conquest on were designed as the private residence of a man of authority or wealth.

When the invaders landed in 1066 approximately half of the total force was composed of Normans and the rest were a mixture of French, Bretons and other nationals. Naturally these men expected some reward for their support of William, and the most usual arrangement was that land was distributed more or less in accordance with the man's importance or the size of his contribution to the invasion. The larger landowners, the tenants-in-chief, were given a number of holdings or manors, which might be scattered over the country or grouped together to form a *"castellaria"* within the proximity of the headquarters or main castle. In return for the land the lord was expected to support the king with his troops; this system of exchanging land for protection was the basis of the feudal system in this country, although the continental systems varied in detail. The tenant was expected to serve with the king's army

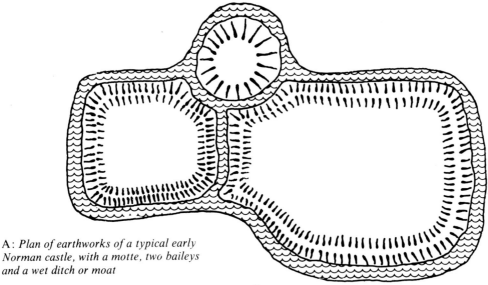

A: *Plan of earthworks of a typical early Norman castle, with a motte, two baileys and a wet ditch or moat*

5

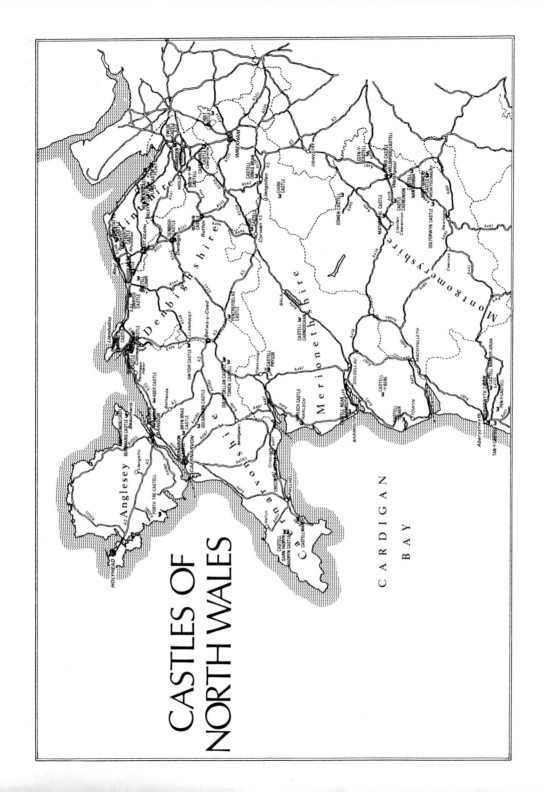

CASTLES OF
NORTH WALES

for a period, normally forty days, should he be called upon by the king or his tenant-in-chief. He could also be called on to serve as castle guard. This system worked very well to start with, but as time passed problems arose. It was feasible for a minor or a woman to inherit the estate, in which case they were obviously useless as far as discharging their obligations in war or guard duties were concerned. To overcome this situation there arose the system of "scutage", whereby a sum of money was paid which then relieved the tenant of the duty to serve. Scutage was collected and used to hire mercenaries to serve with the army or to act as castle guards.

In the years immediately following the Conquest it was essential that the castle should be erected quickly; the situation was potentially very hazardous since the Normans were in a rebellious countryside which might rise against them at any time. The castle had to be simple and capable of being erected very quickly and, almost invariably, the earliest Norman castles were of the motte and bailey type. They were scattered over the countryside at strategic points, and at least one hundred were erected in the first half century. With the aid of pressed peasantry a deep circular ditch was dug and the excavated earth thrown into the centre to form a mound, the "motte"; the top of this was flattened and on it was erected a simple wooden palisade. At first the main defence was simply a wooden fence but, no doubt, a wooden lookout tower and some form of dwelling were soon added. At the base of the motte was another open space also encircled by some form of ditch, and this area was known as the "bailey". There might be one, two or even three, and each might be encircled with a ditch. The earth excavated was used to erect a small defensive wall or rampart around the edge of the bailey. Not every castle had an artificial motte, for if some natural feature, a crag, a mound or a hill could be used then time and labour were saved by building the palisade at the top of such a feature. The most immediate and greatest potential danger to such castles was, of course, fire. In order to overcome this hazard the wooden defences were replaced as soon as possible with masonry; indeed, in one or two cases of important castles such as the Tower of London, the castle was actually built with masonry *ab initio*.

Despite popular belief, castle building was rigidly controlled and it was normal for application to be made to the king for permission to build a castle, in which case a "licence to crenellate" was granted. This procedure was normally followed although during periods of stress, such as the civil wars of Stephen's reign (1135–1154), numbers of so-called "adulterine" castles were erected without permission. When Henry II came to the throne in 1154 he destroyed large numbers of these castles.

Apart from the introduction of masonry walls another very important feature of early 12th Century castles was the introduction of the great stone tower. These were not exclusive to the 12th Century, and there are instances of some earlier than this, but the majority are of this period. The towers vary greatly in detail but they conform to a broad pattern; they are square or rectangular, tall, and the walls are frequently reinforced with small buttresses or pilasters. At the corners were small towers, normally rectangular in shape on the early ones. Such strongholds were known as the "great tower", the "keep" or the "donjon", the latter a term whose meaning has become confused and is now most often used in the sense of a prison. Some cells were often to be found in the keep, but contrary to popular belief they were not in the basement; in practice the majority of castles at which it is known that prisoners were kept have the cells or places of confinement on the upper floors. The base of most keeps are splayed slightly to give greater stability, and also to provide a convenient point of ricochet for any stones dropped from above. To reduce the possibility of men and missiles entering, the lower part of the keep was usually devoid of openings, or else any which existed were very narrow. The main entrance to the keep was normally, but not invariably, on the first floor and approached by a flight of steps set at right angles to the entrance, that is running up the side of the wall. This made it extremely difficult for attackers to build up momentum when using anything like a battering ram to break down the door. It also reduced the number of attackers able to assault the door at any one time simply by the physical limitations of space. Sometimes the motte was of insufficient strength to support these heavy masses of masonry and extra foundations were put in; in other cases the keep was erected on a different site. The internal arrangements of the keep varied but, in general, the large chambers were divided by cross walls and access to the various floors was obtained by stairs set within the thickness of the wall or spiral staircases fitted into the

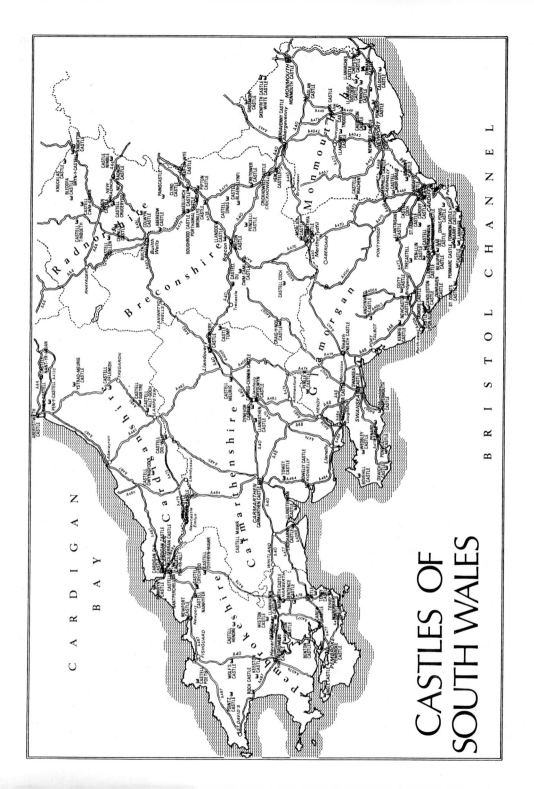

# CASTLES OF SOUTH WALES

corner turrets. The entrance was often given extra protection by the construction of a forebuilding which might include other means of defence such as a drawbridge or a portcullis.

A variation on the large, rectangular keep was known as a "shell keep". These are more often found on the top of the original motte and consist of a large, circular wall which replaced the original wooden palisade. On the inside of the wall were built the kitchens, the buttery, the larder, the store houses, the smithy, a chapel and a hall. Frequently these inside buildings were of wood and in many cases no trace of them has survived; in others the buildings were of stone, and many of these have survived in various degrees.

The baileys, too, were surrounded by masonry walls, and a lesson which the military architect soon learnt was that the wall had to be covered by some form of flanking fire. To this end small projecting towers were spaced along the wall so that archers might loose arrows at any attackers who had managed to reach the foot of the wall. Entrances to the bailey, which were potentially a point of weakness, were normally given extra protection in the form of a strong gatehouse, often with forward works, known as the "barbican". These usually had one or more portcullises, double doors and long passageways through which any attacker had to pass, during which time he was subject to attack from above by means of openings in the roof known as "murder holes". The vast majority of castles were very well equipped to resist attack and very few of them were carried by storm; the majority of victories came as a result of starvation or treachery.

Against the castle every means of attack could be and was employed. Basically the attacker had four possibilities: through, over or under the wall, or starvation brought on by a long siege. To get over the wall there was the scaling ladder, difficult to use since the wall might be twenty to thirty feet high and to get to the foot of the wall a moat, either wet or dry, had to be crossed. It was also essential to use large numbers of ladders to enable a maximum number of men to attack at once. The moat had to be filled with debris or bridged, during which time the attackers were at the mercy of the defenders. The siege tower could be used; this timber, wheeled staging was erected on the site and wheeled into position against the wall. When a drawbridge was lowered from the top of the tower to the top of the wall, the attackers could rush over. Breaking through the wall was normally attempted by means of artillery in the form of catapults of various kinds. There were the trebuchet and the mangonel, both of which could be used to hurl heavy stones against the points of weakness, usually the corner of a tower or the junction of walls. Slower and more hazardous was the pick, which was a battering ram with a sharpened end, the object being to break away stones and achieve some form of breach. The battering ram might be used against doorways but against masonry walls it was relatively useless. Possibly the most effective means of direct attack was under the wall by means of a mine; in this process a tunnel was dug until the foundations of the tower—normally the corner, the weakest point—were reached. These were chipped away or burrowed under and the masonry supported on wooden props. The space was then filled with all manner of inflammable material—straw, pitch, bacon fat, carcasses, etc.—and, at an arranged time, the debris was ignited. As the flames burnt through the wooden props support for the entire weight of masonry was suddenly removed and the corner of the tower would drag itself down. This method was employed very successfully at Rochester, and later repairs are indicated by the fact that the original square tower was replaced by a round one.

One of the features of Edwardian castles was the adoption of this rounded tower, which had several military advantages; it reduced the number of blind points, it removed the dangerous corners which were always points of weakness, and also it was geometrically better able to deflect boulders and other projectiles. The first rounded towers were probably made very late in the 12th Century or very early in the 13th; the first ones were solid and possibly could be described better as bastions. A "D"-shaped tower had many of the same advantages, and was cheaper than a round one.

In addition to the main entrance to the castle there were often a number of postern gates, which were small and so placed that a raiding party from inside might slip out but the gate itself was not vulnerable to an outside attack. A feature which was probably borrowed from France was the machicolation; these were parapets, often quite narrow, built projecting above an entrance, with holes let

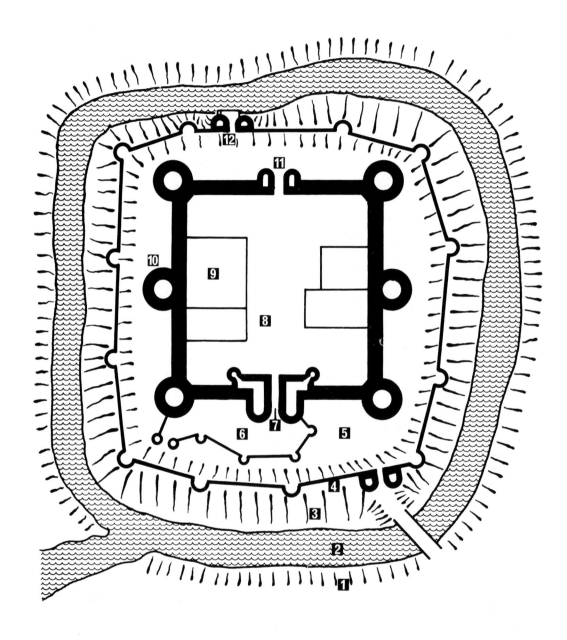

into the floor. These looked down directly on the wall beneath so that the defender could pour boiling water, burning tar or any other objectionable material directly down on the heads of the attackers. Sometimes in place of the more elaborate machicolations a simple enclosed wooden platform, known as a brattice, was fitted into place on a series of wooden beams let into holes in the wall. The simplest defence for the wall walks of a castle were crenellations—popularly, battlements—the pierced stone parapets which allowed defenders to avoid undue exposure. Often these were fitted with heavy wooden shutters which could be closed over the gaps or embrasures to present an unbroken wall to the attackers, at need.

During the 13th and 14th Centuries the emphasis began to shift away from the massive keep. While it could be made almost impregnable it had certain disadvantages from a military point of view; it forced the defenders to adopt a relatively passive approach, gave the attackers the initiative, and by its very lack of easy entrances and exits was comparatively simple to blockade. Many castles built in the late 13th and early 14th Centuries featured greatly strengthened outer defences. Several main towers, linked by strong walls guarded by projecting towers at regular intervals, offered a more flexible defence. The keep could remain as the last citadel, but the greater area defended could be used to accommodate both men and livestock. In practice the attacker still had to concentrate on one or two major points of assault, so the defender was not forced to spread his garrison thinly—while the greater length of defended wall presented problems for the besieger attempting to establish a tight blockade. The number of smaller towers spaced along the walls proliferated, allowing enfilading fire to be brought down on attackers at any point. The individual strength of these towers increased, until many were small self-contained fortresses which might hold out even when the curtain wall on either side had fallen to the attacker, representing a continuing threat to his flanks and rear.

The ingenuity displayed by the castle-builders of Britain in the early 14th Century, as each new technique of defensive design learned from the Continent, the Middle East, or local conflicts was incorporated, reached its peak in the great concentric castles which sprang up in the wake of Edward I's campaigns. An outer curtain of massive walls with strong towers and a complex barbican encircled an inner ring of defences as strong as the first, with the gatehouse off-set some distance from the outer barbican. The two rings of defence were often quite close, with the inner ring at the top of a slope. Thus attackers were faced initially by two banks of defenders; and even if the outer curtain was penetrated and all its towers subdued—no easy task—the space between the curtains became little more than a killing-ground. The castle itself was as strong as ever, with huge round or polygonal towers to defy the most energetic mining, and the layout of the defences often rendered mining of the inner ring or the keep impossibly difficult. With such sophisticated fortifications, castles were often defended successfully by surprisingly small garrisons.

In the early 14th Century the appearance of a weapon new to the West forced a great deal of re-thinking on the matter of castle design. Firearms made their appearance in Europe at about this time and it is known for certain that they were here by 1326. Their possession gave the king a considerable advantage for, as a rule, he alone possessed the facilities to produce gunpowder in bulk; but the advent of cannon meant that even the most powerful defences could be breached. When the handgun developed this too had a minor effect on design, since the arrow slits which had been cut into the wall for the archer were normally vertical and, although narrow, enabled the archer to cover a wide arc of fire. In order to give the gunner the same ability to traverse his weapon cross-slits had to be added to produce the cruciform slits. Embrasures "splayed" on the outside, to allow traversing, also appeared.

B: *Simplified plan of a typical concentric castle built on a natural hillock, with outer earthwork defences:*
1. *counterscarp*  2. *moat or wet ditch*
3. *scarp and berm*
4. *outer curtain, with open-backed towers*
5. *outer bailey*
6. *barbican*  7. *gatehouse*
8. *inner bailey*
9. *great hall*
10. *towers on inner curtain, linked by wall walks and passages*
11. *rear gatehouse*
12. *postern*

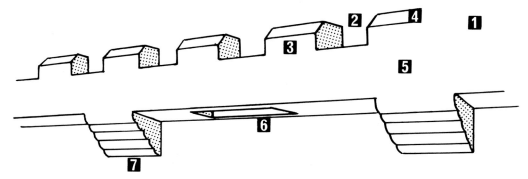

C: *Defensive structures on a castle wall:*
(1) *battlements, crenellation* (2) *crenel or embrasure* (3) *merlon* (4) *chamfer on merlon* (5) *parapet* (6) *machicolation* (7) *corbel*

As military necessity declined in England there was less emphasis placed on defence and more on comfort. By the 15th Century the majority of new buildings, while having some defensive features, were primarily designed for comfortable living conditions, and castles such as Tattershall were the latest style. Earlier strongholds were gradually modified, or abandoned outright and replaced by great houses of a richer and more relaxed style nearby. The construction of fortified houses steadily declined during the 15th Century; and in the 16th Century, in general, the only form of castles built or developed were those intended for coastal defence, specifically designed to mount artillery. Henry VIII built large numbers of these along the south coast to ward off attack from France, and Elizabeth I maintained them against the Spaniards. Castles briefly regained some of their importance during the Civil Wars of the 17th Century. Many were held as important strongholds of Parliamentary or Royalist forces, and suffered repeated attacks. Despite isolated epics of endurance, their ancient fabric and design had now been outstripped by the developing technology of firearms; even those which survived Cromwell's cannon did not long survive his engineers, for it became established policy for the victorious troops of the Lord Protector to "slight" captured castles—that is, to destroy their defensive value by partial demolition. It is surprising how soon many castles decayed, considering the massive solidity of their structure, but the records of repairs and reconstructions show clearly that in a comparatively short period a castle could fall into a very considerable state of disrepair. When abandoned they could quickly be reduced to rubble by local people using them as convenient sources of dressed stone and other building materials.

Despite their decline, the castles of Britain had established themselves firmly in national folklore, and many wealthy gentlemen of the 18th and 19th Centuries fed their pretensions by christening their newly-built houses "the Castle" or "the Towers". (This practice had its valuable side—for it was this tide of rather ill-informed romanticism which eventually led to the first serious efforts to preserve and restore many ruined castles for the interest of posterity.) Some even paid for the erection of "sham" castles, stark ruins in a "ready aged" condition, with no other function than to lend glamour to an imposing landscape—or to the estates of some *nouveau riche* magnate.

In the rugged North and West fortified residences were a practical necessity long after the southern and central areas of Britain had lapsed into comparative peace. In Scotland clan warfare persisted, and apart from the great Norman castles of the Middle Ages and the splendid baronial piles of the 16th to 19th Centuries, a more modest type of castle was still to be found in great numbers. These stark tower-houses were the strongholds of chieftains and landowners of every degree, their sophistication or lack of it reflecting the different levels of wealth and power of their lords. At their greatest, they were rebuilt or enlarged over the centuries to bring them closer into line with the mainstream of castle design, but often retained signs of their earlier simplicity. At their most modest, they were simply plain stone towers with attached halls and projecting turrets, which could be defended against feuding clansmen or border reivers by a relatively small number of bowmen or musketeers. Most of them ran little risk of attack with heavy artillery; their structure was adequate to hold off the comparatively small and lightly armed war parties of the day, and they were threatened by starvation, surprise assaults and treachery more than by advanced engineering techniques. The same conditions governed the emergence of many of the smaller strongholds in Wales. The Norman penetrations brought some of the greatest castles in Britain to the western mountains and estuaries, but there were also many simpler fortresses which had features in common with the Scots pattern. The holds of Welsh chiefs and obscure Norman frontier lords rose according to wealth or manpower, often on sites of great natural strength and sometimes utilizing the foundations of earthworks of earlier Roman and Celtic settlements.

## GLOSSARY OF TERMS

T HE following is a glossary of some of the most common terms connected with the structure of castles and siege warfare which occur in the body of the text:

**bailey:** defended courtyard or ward of a castle

**ballista:** early missile weapon resembling large crossbow on portable carriage, firing metal bolts, arrows or stone slugs

**balustrade:** ornamental parapet of posts and railing

**barbican:** fortified outwork defending gate of a castle or town

**barmkin:** Scottish term for defended courtyard of a castle, often rather smaller than conventional ward or bailey; possibly a corruption of "barbican". Also, the wall enclosing such an area

**bartizan:** overhanging corner turret

**belfry:** siege tower; wooden tower mounted on wheels or rollers, often covered with wet hides as protection against fire, which could be pushed against the wall of a besieged castle. Many had drop-bridges at the top, so that attackers could fight their way across on to the towers or wall walks

**berm:** flat area between base of wall and edge of ditch or moat

**bratticing:** wooden housing erected on top of walls, sometimes with machicolations (*qv*). When erected on top of towers, sometimes also known as "war-head"

**bore:** iron-tipped battering ram for attacking masonry, also known as pick

**castellation:** battlements, implying use as decorative feature

**chamfer:** bevelled face formed by cutting off corner of stone or timber structure

**constable:** title of governor of castle: also warden, captain, castellan

**corbel:** projecting stone (or timber) feature on a wall to support an overhanging parapet, platform, turret, etc.

**crenellation:** fortification—a "licence to crenellate" was official permission to raise a fortified building or fortify an existing structure. The "crenel" was the gap or embrasure in the battlements along a wall

**curtain:** wall enclosing a bailey, courtyard, or ward

**donjon:** keep or great tower, the main citadel of a castle of the 11th and 12th Centuries. The corruption "dungeon", in the sense of a prison cell, has little basis in fact

**embrasure:** see *crenellation*

**enceinte:** enclosure or courtyard

**forebuilding:** projecting defensive work screening entrance of keep or other structure from direct attack

**garderobe:** latrine

**hoarding:** wooden shuttering fitted to parapet of wall as extra protection for defenders

**keep:** see *donjon*

**machicolation:** openings in floor of projecting parapet or platform along wall or above archway, through which defenders could drop or shoot missiles vertically on attackers below

**mangonel:** siege engine for hurling heavy stones

**merlon:** the "teeth" of battlements, between the crenels or embrasures

**motte:** artificial (or improved natural) mound on which castle was built. "Motte and bailey" implies crude 11th Century defence comprising simple timber palisade on top of earth mound, with or without buildings inside

**murder holes:** openings in the roofs of passageways, especially entrances, through which attackers could be ambushed

**parapet:** protective wall on outer side of wall walk

**pit prison:** underground cell, with access through hatch in ceiling only. Also known sometimes as "bottle dungeons", from their shape in section

**portcullis:** heavy wooden, iron, or combination grille protecting an entrance, either in isolation or combined with a conventional door; raised and lowered by winches in gatehouse

**postern:** small door or gate, usually some distance from main entrance of castle or ward. Often obscure or actually hidden, they enabled defenders to slip in and out of a castle, without being vulnerable to major attacks. If specifically designed to enable surprise flank attacks on besiegers, known as "sallyports"

**solar:** private living quarters of lord, usually adjacent to great hall

**turning bridge:** early variation on drawbridge, operating on "see-saw" principle

**yett:** Scottish variation on portcullis—gate made of intersecting iron bars penetrating each other vertically and horizontally. This formidable defence was ultimately banned

## A BRIEF CHRONOLOGY OF WELSH MILITARY HISTORY

The castles of Wales are now awesome ruins evocative of the romantic age of medieval battles, of knights, sieges, and heroic bids for power and independence. They are also grim reminders of treachery, oppression and lost causes. Impassively, they record in enduring stone the most important years of Wales's history.

The true period of castle-building covered the years between the Norman conquest of the 11th Century and the Wars of the Roses in the mid-15th Century, but the years immediately before and after this period were also significant. The first people to experience the fierce resistance of Wales, and to discover the necessity for a system of fortresses and secure communications were the Romans, under Scapula, who invaded South Wales

*A.D. 49: Romans invade South Wales*

in A.D. 49. Despite the relatively rapid subjugation of southern Britain, the Celts of the west and north (the Welsh share distant ancestry with the Scots and Irish) vigorously resisted pacification for almost 30 years. Three hundred years later the Roman troops finally sailed away to defend other frontiers of the crumbling empire; and a century of attempted or actual minor invasions of the high country of western Britain ensued.

*383–410: Roman rule in Britain comes to an end*

The departure of the legions left the island without unity or leadership, and dozens of chieftains split the country into minor factions which only united in the face of invasion from common enemies such as the Picts and

490: *Saxons defeated by Arthur*

590: *Orthodox Christianity brought to England, isolating Wales*

757–796: *Offa rules in Mercia; Welsh stabilise border*

851: *Danish attacks on Britain begin. Rhodri Mawr saves Wales*

1067: *Normans enter South Wales under FitzOsbern*

1087: *William the Conqueror dies in France and is succeeded by William II*

Saxons—and not always then. The southern central and western areas of Britain put up a fierce resistance to the incursion of Saxon raiders and settlers from across the North Sea, however, and from this sparsely recorded period there are echoes of great victories which held up the spread of the Saxons for 50 years. The legendary name of Arthur is closely woven into these almost forgotten chronicles.

The Welsh language began to emerge in the 5th and 6th Centuries, and the age of the Christian missionaries followed, with Wales's patron saint David spreading the preaching of his austere faith from his monastery in south-west Wales. The country became religiously isolated after Augustine landed in England from Rome, and in the 7th and 8th Centuries Welsh hopes of influencing England died. From that point on it was a matter of protecting national independence against constant pressure from the English. Any westward expansion met determined resistance; and when Offa, King of Mercia in the English border lands, built his great dyke or earthwork from the north coast of Wales to the river Wye in the south, it may have been intended as much to keep the Welsh out as to justify the abandonment of attempts to push his frontier westwards. To this day a great deal of the dyke can be traced, and the present borders are not remarkably different.

The Danish Vikings posed a new and unexpected threat when they attacked Wales along its largely undefended west coast. The Welsh found a leader in Rhodri Mawr—Rhodri the Great—who not only drove out the Danes but also brought an end to the constant internal squabbling and a greater degree of unity than Wales had known since the days of the Romans. After his death, however, Wales once again split into three regions, rendering itself vulnerable to the Normans and the "new" English.

The expansion of the Normans into Wales in the years following the conquest of England by William the Bastard was no easier a task than the Romans and Saxons had faced. FitzOsbern and his knights only achieved a measure of success by making a number of limited thrusts, consolidated immediately by the most thorough programme of castle-building yet seen in the British Isles. William the Conqueror, his son William Rufus, and Henry I after him found that the problem of Wales required the attention of their hardiest and most able followers—such as William FitzOsbern, Earl of Hereford in the south, and Roger Montgomery and Hugh of Avranches in the north. Determined as the Welsh were, they were no match for Norman mail,

Marcher Lords established on Welsh borders

1100: *Henry I comes to the throne of England*

Norman domination spreads

Norman bishops replace Welsh at St. David's

1135: *Henry I dies; England wracked by civil wars between Stephen and Matilda*

Owain Gwynedd drives Normans from North Wales

1154: *Henry II crowned Rhys ap Gruffydd rises to power in South Wales*

Norman castles, and the Norman skill at warfare, ingrained into this uniquely energetic race of wanderers over generations of hard experience. Gradually the imposition of the feudal system increased the number of castles and the number of villagers sheltering under their walls. The Lords Marcher became powerful – indeed, almost autonomous – rulers of the border lands; and the Welsh, whose culture had never included permanent towns such as those established by the Normans, withdrew further and further into their forbidding mountains.

The 35-year reign of Henry I was a grim period for the Welsh. Foreigners in a hostile land, the Normans strengthened their timber strongholds with stone walls and keeps, and built more castles which became the focal points of yet more settlements. Pembrokeshire and the Vale of Glamorgan became so populated with English and Normans that Welsh was heard less and less, and a part of Pembrokeshire became known as "Little England beyond Wales". The border of this area, the "Landsker", is still apparent. Nearby Gerald de Windsor held Pembroke Castle in Henry's name, and the estuaries and inlets of Milford Haven gave the sea-going foreigners easy access into the heart of South Wales. St. John and St. Peter edged out St. David and St. David's itself was the seat of a Norman bishop when the supremacy of Canterbury overshadowed its influence as a religious centre.

Welsh relief at the death of the able and determined Henry I in 1135 was followed by elation at the opportunities for Welsh gains which were offered by the bitter wrangling over the succession to the English throne. The Marcher Lords sided with the Empress Matilda, and Welsh leaders seized their chance eagerly. Owain Gwynedd's supporters in the north drove out many of the intruders, clearing the land of Normans almost as far as Chester. Most of the south—with the solidly Norman exception of Pembrokeshire—also rose against the occupiers. Stephen, embroiled in the problems of England, unintentionally gave Wales a vital breathing space; had he been as strong as his successor Henry II, it is unlikely that the cause of Welsh nationalism would have survived his reign. Powerful as Henry II was, even he could not crush the spirit of a country which had tasted freedom once again.

In the south arose a leader who was to make this region as strong as the north, despite the years of Norman supremacy—Rhys ap Gruffydd, whose seat was at Dynevor Castle. Henry II was no more ready to tolerate independence than his great namesake had been; in

*1165: Welsh unite to defeat Henry's army*

*Wales again divided*

*1175: Welsh regain territories*

*1188–92: Giraldus Cambrensis writes his "Itinerary" and "Description of Wales"*

*1189: Richard I (Lionheart) crowned. Beginning of Third Crusade*
*Rise of Llywelyn ap Iorwerth—"the Great"*

1165 he gathered a huge army from England and his French territories, intending to snuff out Welsh resistance for all time. As always when threatened from outside, the Welsh united; and Owain Gwynedd, Rhys ap Gruffydd, and Owain Cyfeiliog of Powys brought together the biggest host that Wales had ever seen. Henry's army began to cross the desolate mountains of the Berwyns in central Wales, around Corwen. Strong as the Welsh army was, it seemed that it would melt before the invaders; but with perfect timing, a violent storm broke. Burdened by its baggage train, hampered by its armour and engines, and confused by the strange surrounding, the unwieldy English army was no match for the Welsh and the elements combined. The windswept bogs 2,000 feet above sea level saw Henry's hopes founder as dismally as his soldiers.

Once again, however, Welsh unity broke down as soon as the immediate threat was removed. Rhys and Owain Gwynedd turned on Owain Cyfeiliog, throwing away their last chance to build a unified country. Though Henry had been beaten in one campaign, his strength could not be ignored, and in time both these powerful leaders had to come to terms with him. Nevertheless, Owain Gwynedd had secured the north against outright invasion, and gradually the Welsh regained much of their lands. Henry II treated Rhys, in the south, with considerable respect, and a period of calm returned to Wales. It was now that Rhys held the first gathering of the bards, at Cardigan in 1177, setting the pattern for the Eisteddfodds of the future.

For Wales, the end of the 12th Century was vastly different from its beginning. It had dawned with fresh memories of the Norman occupation and the expectation of a dismal future under Henry I; it ended with recovery of territory, pride of achievement, and recognition in new fields brought about by the writer, historian, ecclesiastic and traveller Giraldus Cambrensis. The tales of Merlin, Arthur and Camelot, and the prophecy of Welsh glory under a Welsh king were enthusiastically elaborated, and given a veneer of authenticity, by the haphazard and imaginative historian Geoffrey of Monmouth. There was another reason why Welsh hearts were buoyant with hope and confidence— once again the north had produced a leader, one even greater than Owain Gwynedd. This was Llywelyn ap Iorwerth, who would be surnamed the Great. He began as ruler of Gwynedd, and extended his influence over an ever increasing area of Wales while Richard I of England—"the Lionheart"—was absent on the Crusade.

1199: *John succeeds to English throne*

1215: *Magna Carta—new Welsh rights recognised and territories recovered*

1216: *Henry III succeeds to English throne*

1240: *Dispute over the succession to Llywelyn the Great*

1258: *Llywelyn ap Gruffydd seizes power in Wales*

*Henry III recognises Llywelyn as Prince of Wales*

1272: *Edward I succeeds to the throne of England*

Llywelyn increased his power by taking advantage of the conflict between the next English king, John, and his barons; eventually he joined the baronial revolt, thus winning recognition of many Welsh rights in the Magna Carta.

Llywelyn was not so blinded by patriotism that he could not form some idea of the probable future, or fail to see the strength of his past and future enemies. He tried to create a central authority as the first step to unity, and encouraged a change from the old tribal and pastoral patterns to the feudal and manorial style demonstrated by the Normans. Llywelyn, despite siding with the barons, had married John's daughter, a fact which doubtless contributed to his success as much as the distraction of Richard and the weakness of John. He was an excellent leader and organiser, worthy of his title, and when Henry III came to the throne he was well advised by his court to recognise Llywelyn's power in Wales. Llywelyn in his turn recognised the ultimate sovereignty of Henry, as he had of John.

Llywelyn the Great died in 1240, having erred in one vital respect—the appointment of a strong successor. In Llywelyn's case, he had disowned his son Gruffydd and his grandson Llywelyn ap Gruffydd, for not recognising the English kings, and his death resulted in considerable dispute. Henry III could have used this period of uncertainty to assert himself in Wales, but by this time he too was having trouble with his barons. Llywelyn ap Gruffydd eventually seized power and styled himself "Prince of Wales". He had followed his far-sighted grandfather in allying himself with the English barons, and was particularly close to Simon de Montfort, the powerful leader of the baronial opposition to Henry. At the Treaty of Montgomery, Henry III was compelled to recognise Llywelyn and his title; so Llywelyn ap Gruffydd became the first, and only, recognised native Prince of Wales, and continued the administrative reforms of his grandfather. To the Welsh it must have appeared that independence was secured.

The Prince was not without enemies, however, and nor was he above making mistakes. His greatest mistake was underestimating Edward I, one of the most formidable monarchs ever to wear a crown. The presence of unruly independent states on his borders simply did not fit in with Edward's concept of kingship—as both Wales and Scotland were to discover to their cost. Adding insult to injury, Llywelyn married the daughter of Simon de Montfort, the rebel baron whose army Edward, as Prince Edward, had defeated in 1265. He also refused to

1274: *Llywelyn refuses to attend Edward's coronation*

1277: *Llywelyn attacks border areas; Edward invades Wales.*

*Llewelyn sues for peace. Treaty of Rhuddlan signed, and first Edwardian castles are begun*

1282: *Llywelyn and Dafydd attack the English, and Edward invades for second time*

1282: *Llywelyn is killed, Dafydd seeks refuge, and resistance collapses*

attend Edward's coronation or his Parliament at Westminster; to do so would have been to pay homage to the king, and to recognise his supremacy. For Edward there could be only one answer; when Llywelyn made attacks on the border regions in 1277 he was formally declared a rebel, and the English army marched into Wales. Edward attacked from Chester, Montgomery and Carmarthen, and soon Llywelyn was confined to the mountain fastnesses of the north, despite fierce resistance. The English moved rapidly along the coasts, and then Edward brought his fleet into play; he cut off Anglesey, the supply base and potential refuge of the northern chieftains and their Prince. Llywelyn had no option but to sue for peace, and before the year was out the harsh terms of the treaty were signed at Rhuddlan Castle. Llywelyn was allowed to keep his title, but it was a meaningless princedom—little territory went with it, and no authority over other Welsh leaders.

This was Edward's mistake; he in his turn had made as faulty an assessment of the Welsh as Llywelyn had made of him. The Welsh, without a leader except one they did not know or want, watched with fear and loathing as the great castles rose like blisters in Edward's wake—Aberystwyth, Flint, Rhuddlan, Builth, and huge new works on the sites of older castles and captured Welsh strongholds. By 1282 Wales had lapsed once more into that state of fractious disorder which required only a spark to set off another full scale revolt. Llywelyn's brother Dafydd struck the spark by seizing Hawarden Castle; the uprising spread instantly through central and northern Wales, and the Prince of Wales threw his support behind his brother. Initially the rebels were successful, capturing Flint and Rhuddlan and pressing on towards Chester. But once again the grim King of England marshalled his army and launched a three-pronged assault overland, supported by his fleet—every major castle that Edward built, except Builth alone, could be provisioned from the sea.

Almost immediately the Welsh began to lose ground. Llywelyn tried to raise support in the south from his base at Aberedw Castle, but was rejected by the garrison at Builth. On his way to rejoin his supporters and return to the north, the Prince of Wales ran into a group of English soldiers and was killed. For a while Dafydd struggled to keep the rebellion alive, but it was a futile hope. He was betrayed and captured, declared a traitor, and in 1283 was hung, drawn and quartered at Shrewsbury. The bid for independence died as suddenly as it had been born; and a second group of Edwardian castles, even more

19

*1283-1300: Four more Edwardian castles are built. First shires are formed in north*

*(1307: Edward II)*
*(1327: Edward II!)*
*(1377: Richard II)*
*(1399: Henry IV)*

*1400: Uprising led by Owain Glyndwr*

*1402: Henry IV unable to quell Welsh rebellion*

*1403: Sir Henry Percy—"Hotspur" —is killed while supporting Glyndwr. Rebels hold most of Wales*

*French support Welsh; French fleet in Irish Sea*

colossal, rose to tower over the defeated Welsh at Caernarvon, Harlech, Conway, and later at Beaumaris, while towns huddled inside new battlemented walls. At Rhuddlan Edward wrote the administrative and legislative chapters of his conquest, and out of Llywelyn's principality formed the English-style shires of Anglesey, Caernarvon, Flint, Cardigan and Merioneth. The rest of the troublesome areas remained under the rule of the powerful Marcher Lords, and the administrative shape of Wales was set for the next two and a half centuries. Wales settled down to a long period of strange, uneasy calm disturbed only by isolated skirmishes.

The peace was suddenly and violently shattered by the revolt of Owain Glyndwr, immortalised by his own actions and by Shakespeare's *"Owen Glendower"*. Glyndwr rose to a position of influence at exactly the right time to take advantage of the unrest of the peasants of England and Wales, and of Henry IV's preoccupation with maintaining his tenuous grip on the crown, which he had claimed after forcing Richard II to abdicate in 1399. When a group of Welsh rebels pronounced Owain Glyndwr the "rightful Prince of Wales", the flames of rebellion spread through Wales as fast as the fire spread through Ruthin, the first town attacked by Glyndwr. Henry rushed troops to Wales and almost crushed the revolt; but with the vicious anti-Welsh legislation which he forced through Parliament he aroused native fury to an even greater height, and by 1402 the revolt was once more in full swing. Henry tried to invade Wales and subdue Glyndwr, but, like another Henry advancing on another Owain 300 years before, he was thwarted by violent weather. To Glyndwr's heroic image there was now added the reputation of wizardry, and of being summoned by higher powers. There were few Welsh who doubted that their saviour had arrived, and one after another English strongholds fell to the rebels in every part of Wales. The powerful Percy family, led by "Harry Hotspur"—Sir Henry Percy—aligned themselves with Glyndwr; but even their defeat and "Hotspur's" death at the hands of Henry and his son—the true Prince of Wales—at Shrewsbury in 1403 did not slow down the impetus of the revolt. The most powerful Marcher Lord, Edmund Mortimer, had been captured by the Welsh, and before long Wales belonged to Owain Glyndwr from the Severn to the Mersey. The French also allied themselves with the rebels, and a French fleet in the Irish Sea crushed the last hopes of the English garrisons isolated on the coast. Aberystwyth, Harlech and Criccieth fell, while in the east French and Welsh soldiers marched together as far as Worcester.

Yet the revolt of Owain Glyndwr was to fail as completely as those before it. There was no one dramatic reverse, rather a gradual loss of impetus. In England Henry and his son doggedly persisted, and crushed their rebellious barons one by one. The castles of Wales were retaken, one by one; and in 1410 Glyndwr was forced to go into hiding, moving from one refuge to another as his hunters grew nearer. Eventually, he simply disappeared. Henry V, new to the throne, proclaimed a free pardon for the Welshman, but no word of answer was sent, and the prince who hoped to be King of Wales was never heard of again. Legends proliferated, but all chose to ignore the theory that he took refuge with his son-in-law, Sir John Scudamore, near Bacton in Herefordshire. Owain Glyndwr left a Wales bruised and resentful, hating the English and hated in return; on the face of it he had lost far more than he had won; but he had woken the spirit of nationalism which was to find such fulfilment 75 years later when a son of Wales sat at last on the English throne.

The castles which had been so violently awakened after the inactivity of the 14th Century were now repaired, and those lords who clearly saw the war clouds gathering about the houses of York and Lancaster looked to their walls and moats once again. Raglan, the last great castle to be built in Wales, rose impressively. The Wars of the Roses held interest for the great majority of the Welsh only because of the man who ended them—Henry Tudor, claimant to the Duchy of Lancaster, born in Pembroke Castle. (The Tudors—Tewdwr—came from Anglesey, and Owain Glyndwr was an ancestor. Owain Tudor became the lover of Henry V's widow. A son of theirs, Edmund, married Margaret Beaufort, a descendant of John of Gaunt, Duke of Lancaster; and Henry Tudor was their son. Henry's uncle, Jasper Tudor, Earl of Pembroke, was the half-brother of Henry VI.) It was natural that when Henry returned from exile as the Duke of Lancaster, claimant to the English throne and determined to heal once and for all the rift between York and Lancaster, he should land at Milford Haven and begin his march from Pembroke Castle. With the powerful magnate of South Wales, Sir Rhys ap Thomas, Henry mustered the army which defeated King Richard III on Bosworth Field. A "Welshman" was at last King of England and Wales.

The final chapter in the story of the castles of Wales is that of the Civil War. The period of the Tudor dynasty was, naturally, a contented one for the Welsh, and the

*1410: Revolt collapses and Glyndwr disappears*

*1413: Henry V—Henry of Monmouth —succeeds to English throne*

*(1415: Henry V defeats French at Agincourt)*
*(1422: Henry VI succeeds to English throne as infant)*

*1455: Wars of the Roses break out*

*(1461: Edward IV succeeds to throne)*
*(1483: Princes Edward and Richard murdered in Tower of London. Richard III claims throne)*

*1485: Henry Tudor lands at Milford Haven. Rhys ap Thomas pledges loyalty. Richard III defeated and killed at Bosworth Field. Tudor takes throne as Henry VII*

(1509: *Henry VIII*)
(1547: *Edward VI*)
(1553: *Mary I*)
(1558: *Elizabeth I*)
(1603: *James I*)
(1625: *Charles I*)
1642: *Wales supports Royalist cause in Civil War*
1649: *Charles I executed*

1650–51: *Second Civil War. Charles II flees to France. Cromwell slights castles*

Stuarts maintained the recognition that Wales had enjoyed from the Tudors. In return the Stuarts received Welsh loyalty. When the Civil War broke out in 1642 Wales was firmly Royalist, for it lacked the large middle class which elsewhere provided the breeding ground for Puritanism and the Parliamentary party. Almost without exception, the castles of Wales were garrisoned for King Charles. But Cromwell and the cannon of the New Model Army proved invincible; and in many cases the Lord Protector consolidated his power by rendering indefensible—"slighting"—the castles which had defied him. For all too many of the castles of Wales, the last garrisons of all were Parliamentary soldiers armed with crowbars, hammers and powder-charges.

## GLOSSARY OF WELSH WORDS

**M**ANY of the unfamiliar place names, and names given to castles in Wales are more easily remembered if their meaning is known: thus an anonymous *Castell Du* becomes the more meaningful Black Castle. This glossary contains most of the Welsh words which form parts of place and castle names in this book. Reading the descriptions and following directions is also made easier by knowing at least the rudiments of pronunciation. The most frequently met letters likely to cause difficulty are as follows. "*Ll*" is pronounced the same whether at the beginning or in the middle of a word. It is almost impossible to transliterate the sound, which is produced by starting to say a normal *L*, but slowly, breathing out through the mouth at the same time; thus Llanelli sounds something like *ghlanechli*. "*W*" in the middle of a word has a vowel sound like *oo* in *tool*. "*Y*" is usually *ee* as in *teeth*, but sometimes *i* as in *tin*. When between hyphens, as in Pen-y-Castell, it is nearer *u* as in *fur*. "*Dd*" is pronounced as *th*; "*ph*" as *f*; "*f*" as *v*; and "*ch*" is hard, as in *loch*, not as in *charge*.

| | | | |
|---|---|---|---|
| **aber** | river mouth | **carreg** | stone |
| **afon** | river | **castell** | castle |
| **allt** | cliff, side of hill | **cefn** | ridge, back |
| **ap** | son of | **cleddau** | swords |
| **bach, fach** | little | **clwyd** | gate |
| **bran** | crow, raven | **coch, goch** | red |
| **bras** | rich, large | **coed** | wood |
| **bryn** | hill | **crug, grug** | mound |
| **bwlch** | gap, pass in mountains | **cwm** | valley, depression |
| **cae** | closed field, opposite of *maes* | **dinas** | fort |
| **caer, gaer** | fort | **domen, tomen** | burial mound |
| **carn, garn** | hill, prominence | **du** | black |

dyffryn   vale, valley
fach, bach   little
fawr, mawr   big, great
fechan, fychan   small, the lesser
felin, melin   mill
glas   green (of fields) blue (of sea)
goetre   home in the woods (*coed* plus *tre*)
gwaun, waun   moor
hen   old
hendre   homestead in valley used in winter
llan   church (originally, sacred enclosure)
llyn   lake
llys   court or hall
maes   open field, opposite of *cae*
mawr, fawr   big, great

melin, felin   mill
mynydd   mountain
nant   stream, brook
pant   valley, hollow
pen   head, top
rhos   open moor
rhudd   russet, reddish
tomen, domen   burial mound
tre   home, dwelling place, village
waun, gwaun   moor
y, yr   the, of the
yn   in, at
ynys   island
ystrad   flat ground flanking river course, valley

## THE CASTLES OF WALES: A NOTE ON SELECTION

THE 204 castles in this book are described alphabetically under their most common names. They are located to their nearest town or village, and their county. To enable easy location on a map, straight-line mileages and approximate compass bearings from the nearest town are quoted. The maps which accompany the introduction show the castles in relation to main roads in the area. It should be empha-sised that the directions given should be correlated by potential visitors with a good local road map; in many cases these directions will be sufficient on their own, but they are not claimed to be so in every case, especially where the remains are fragmentary and isolated. Where two sites are very close or liable to be confused for some other reason, exact locations are given by National Grid Reference numbers.

Conditions of access to castles are as at the time of going to press. Some castles are not normally open to the public, but permission to view is often given on written application to the Administrator of the site concerned. Many castles consider special conditions for visits by large parties. Except for those sites on common land and listed as "freely accessible", all castles which have set opening hours are closed on Christmas Day and Boxing Day.

The criteria by which entries could be selected for a book on castles are several. The publishers have chosen not to attempt to define the term "castle" according to any technical criterion, such as the relative military and/or residential importance of the original site; in many cases any such judgement must be based on obscure or speculative data. Sites known by documentary evidence or common usage as "—— Castle" or "Castle ——", in English or Welsh, have been included, and all others excluded. It is accepted that this definition requires brief explanatory mention of several sites of pre-Roman or Roman origin which have no claim to the title "castle" except that of local usage.

**Aber Castle,** *Aber, Caernarvonshire. 5 miles east of Bangor, on A55.*

The Mŵd, an artificial mound in Aber, is all that remains of Aber Castle, and this gives the site its second name of Mŵd Castle. Ancient writings refer to a Bangor Castle built in about 1090, and perhaps it was on this site. Llywelyn the Great, the Welsh leader who gained recognition for Wales in the Magna Carta of 1215, either built a new castle here, or strengthened the old one.

The vanished castle played its part in Welsh history by being the place in which Llywelyn ap Gruffydd, Prince of Wales and grandson of Llywelyn the Great, received and declined Edward I's summons to attend his coronation and the Parliament at Westminster. Had he accepted and paid homage to the King, it would have meant the voluntary surrender of Wales' independence—but his refusal led to the conquest of Wales by Edward, the building of the massive Norman castles, and the years of subjugation they symbolised.

**Aberedw Castle,** *Aberedw, Radnorshire. 3 miles south-east of Builth Wells on B4567.*

Here Llywelyn, Prince of Wales, spent his last hours. Though deep in hostile territory, Aberedw Castle was one of his seats and whenever his affairs in the north allowed, Llywelyn used it as his hunting lodge. Such pastimes stopped forever after the great Welsh rebellion of 1282. Llywelyn moved south with a large force, subdued Cardiganshire and set up his headquarters in Aberedw Castle. Although he had lost most of his territory and influence in the harsh peace terms after

Edward's first invasion in 1277, Llywelyn's constant resistance and the aggression started by his brother Dafydd in 1282 made his final defeat an essential step in Edward I's plans for his kingdom. English forces under Edward Mortimer and Roger L'Estrange were sent to surprise and capture the Prince at Aberedw. News of the impending attack got through to Llywelyn, and the Prince decided to go to Builth to try to raise support from the townspeople and from the garrison at Builth Castle, whose governor Llywelyn thought he could influence. But the Prince of Wales was unsuccessful, and left to rejoin his followers. Tradition says that Llywelyn, knowing the English were close, had reversed the shoes on his horse's hooves to lay a false track in the snow. Unfortunately the blacksmith who did the job was a traitor, and told Mortimer of the ruse. Llywelyn, heading back towards Aberedw with only one companion and almost unarmed, rode right into a pursuing band of English soldiers, and was killed by Adam Francton, a common soldier. It was not until the soldiers searched the bodies for loot some time later that the identity of the slain Welshman was realised.

Llywelyn's head was cut off and sent to King Edward at Rhuddlan Castle, and from there it went to London where, following custom, it was exhibited on a stake outside the Tower. His body was buried on a nearby ridge, which is still called Cefn-y-bedd Llywelyn (ridge of Llywelyn's grave), and the dell where he met his death was named Cwm Llywelyn. One legend says that in the dell broom grew in profusion; that Llywelyn, wounded by the soldier's spear, was finished off with a stick of broom—and that no broom has grown in that vicinity ever since.

There is very little left of Aberedw Castle today. It was a small stronghold with four round towers, but the last of its character was destroyed when the old Cambrian Railway, long since closed, was built through the site and its stones used to ballast the track between Aberedw and Llanelwedd.

**Abergavenny Castle,** *Abergavenny, Monmouthshire. At south end of town, off A40.*

Now a rather uninteresting ruin, concealed by ivy and the adjacent more modern mansion, Abergavenny Castle once moved the poet Churchyard to write of its "most goodly towers". The scant remains of two square towers, a round one and a polygonal one, and a gate with a substantial barbican are all that is left after the passage of years and the destruction by Parliamentarian forces in 1645. The traditional motte and bailey castle was founded soon after the Norman invasion of the

*Abergavenny Castle, scene of treachery and murder when a stronghold of the hated Norman William de Braose stood on the site*

11th Century by Hameline de Balun, but the principal ruins belong to the 13th and 14th Centuries.

In 1172, soon after it was built, it was captured from William de Braose by Sytsylt ap Dyferwald, but was soon restored to him—and then came the act of treachery for which the castle is mainly remembered. De Braose invited Sytsylt and his son Geoffrey, the most renowned and powerful chieftains of Powys, to the castle under the pretext of amity and to celebrate Christmas. But the Welsh chieftains were slaughtered by de Braose and his men to avenge the death of his uncle, Henry of Hereford. Friends of the murdered Welshmen took their revenge in turn—they attacked the castle, burnt it, and captured the governor, his wife, and the whole garrison. Nor was this an isolated act of infamy, for William, son of the Earl of Hereford, did an identical thing in the castle years later.

During the baronial revolt against King John in 1215, Llywelyn ap Iorwerth (the Great) captured the castle from the King's forces, and it narrowly escaped destruction in 1403 when Owain Glyndwr burnt the town during his violent uprising. Until

the Civil War, the castle had a more peaceful existence, with the Barony of Abergavenny being conferred on the possessor of the castle.

**Aberlleiniog Castle,** *Llangoed, Anglesey. 2 miles north Beaumaris off B5109.*

The site of a low motte and bailey castle built in about 1088 by the Earl of Chester. It was captured and destroyed by the Welsh in 1094. The ruined structure on the motte, a small square building with a small tower at each angle, was made with revetted earthwork, and must have been a fortlet built during the Civil War of 1642–52.

**Aberystwyth Castle,** *Aberystwyth, Cardiganshire. On the town's seafront.*

Of the seven remaining castles built by Edward I to enforce his supremacy and his harsh peace terms over Wales, Aberystwyth Castle is the most ruined. Little is left of the towering inner ward, the concentric walls of defence designed and erected by Edward's genius of military engineering, James of St. George. But history remains in abundance.

Aberystwyth was the site of fortifications long before the present ruins were a powerful new castle—Pen Dinas, the hill just south of the town, was crowned by one of the largest Iron Age forts in west Wales. The first Aberystwyth Castle was built south of the present site, in the Ystwyth valley (at Nat. Grid Ref. SN 585790—see Castell Tan-y-castell). It was begun by Gilbert de Clare, one of the Norman lords who moved up the west coast subduing the inhabitants—in this case, Cadgwan in particular. Henry I gave his permission for Gilbert to attack Cardiganshire to settle his dispute with Cadgwan.

As was the usual fate of the modest defences of that time, this castle was repeatedly taken, burnt and rebuilt by the Welsh and the Normans. In 1171 Henry II gave Cardiganshire to Rhys ap Grufydd, the magnate of South Wales. Rhys's sons disputed the succession on his death, Maelgwyn finally seizing his brothers' territory. In 1207, fearing an attack by Llywelyn the Great, Maelgwyn destroyed the castle. Llywelyn came nevertheless, rebuilt the castle and gave it to Rhys and Owen, nephews of Maelgwyn (who was killed after he had once again turned on his family, and joined the English). King John was the next possessor of this castle, having persuaded Rhys and Owen to give up their territories when the rest of Wales was subdued. In 1215 Llywelyn the Great captured Cardigan Castle and Cardiganshire with it, and also took possession of the castle at Aberystwyth. More sieges and changes of possession followed, the English eventually being conquered there by Maelgwyn the younger in 1231, though by then a fortification may have been started on the new site.

Then came Edward I, and the new Aberystwyth Castle on the present site. Like others built in the last quarter of the 13th Century, it was extremely powerful and was one of the major English strongholds in the west. It remained secure until Owain Glyndwr captured it in 1404 during his remarkable uprising. Prince Henry retook it in 1407, Glyndwr held it again briefly, but then the English regained possession in 1408. The castle's next major military event was the Civil War of 1642–46 when it was held for Charles I by Royalists until it surrendered to Colonel Rice Powell in April 1646. In typical fashion Cromwell ordered the castle to be dismantled, a task carried out in 1647.

A selection of coins in the nearby University College Museum recalls a more peaceful stage in the castle's history. Rich silver-ore deposits near the walled town were mined in the 17th Century, and a mint was set up in the castle. Initially the wealth from the mines went to Sir Hugh Myddelton, who was reputed to have earned profits of £25,000 a year from them (a fortune which was largely spent on giving London its first reliable fresh water through the New River project). After Sir Hugh, the mines passed to Thomas Bushell who, being an ardent Royalist, lent much of the resultant wealth to Charles I—and he, being a resourceful ruler, set up the castle mint to turn his borrowings into ready cash. Some of these coins are now in the museum.

Though the castle is now only a ruin, its original massive dimensions can be traced, and the Aberystwyth Corporation has turned the site into pleasant public gardens. From the Castle rock there are striking views of the whole of Cardigan Bay, and on a clear day Snowdon can be seen 44 miles to the north.

# B

**Angle Castle,** *Angle, Pembrokeshire. In village, 8 miles west of Pembroke on B4320.*

The ruins of Angle Castle lie north of the church, and consist only of a single rectangular peel-tower, though it is well-preserved. Nothing is known of its history.

*The much-ruined remains of Aberystwyth Castle, designed by King Edward I's master engineer James of St. George*

**Barry Castle,** *Barry, Glamorgan. On west edge of town, 8 miles south-west of Cardiff.*

The ruins of a small gate or barbican, with adjacent parts of the curtain wall, clad in ivy, are all that is left of this 14th Century fortified manorial residence; and there is no record of its history or of its original appearance.

**Beaumaris Castle,** *Beaumaris, Anglesey. On north edge of town, on B5109.*

After Edward I's second conquest of Wales in 1282, and the death of Llywelyn, the last native Prince of Wales, many Welsh warriors withdrew to Anglesey. To the south, Edward's massive castles at Caernarvon and Conway (both begun in 1283) guarded the entrance to the rest of Wales. But in 1294 a sudden Welsh uprising led by Madoc resulted in Caernarvon Castle being temporarily captured and partly burnt. To strengthen his defence of the Menai Strait and keep the Welsh in check, Edward began the construction of Beaumaris Castle, his last great castle in Wales, in 1295.

The site chosen was low and flat, and if this did not result in a castle with the towering grandeur of some of the others, it certainly gave James of St. George, the Master of the King's Works in Wales, the opportunity to conceive a most attractive design which is a classical example of an extremely strong concentric castle. There is a fine balance and proportion in the almost square inner bailey defended by the towering fifteen-foot-thick walls, with six towers and two powerful gatehouses. That first stage must have been powerful enough—the protruding towers offer excellent flanking defence and the gatehouses could have withstood fierce attack, even without the three portcullises and two doors in each. But about twenty years later an outer bailey was begun, with a thinner, lower, hexagonal curtain wall defended by twelve towers and two gatehouses (though the north gateway was probably never completed). The south gateway guards the dock where the moat met a channel dug through to the sea, and this was also the entrance to the town. The gap between the inner and outer walls is not large, and with the gatehouses in each bailey being offset, Beaumaris Castle would have daunted even the most unimaginative attackers. For the defenders—the castle could hold a large garrison—their tasks were made easier by a mural gallery running within the inner curtain about halfway up, with doorways into the towers and gatehouses, and access to four groups of latrines, one group near each angle. The striking vaulted chapel on the east side of the bailey is near the site of the old racquet court, and the appearance of the castle still maintains its original character.

It is something of an anti-climax that Beaumaris Castle's formidable defences were not put to the test. Perhaps potential attackers realised they would never succeed; perhaps the castle need not have been built at all. At any rate there were few events of any significance in its history until the Civil War, when the castle was garrisoned for Charles I by Thomas, Lord Bulkeley. It was held by the Royalists until 1646, surrendering after Royalist forces were defeated in a nearby battle by a large force of Parliamentarians led by General Mytton. (It is said that one Royalist officer, deciding to swim with the tide, locked his men up in the Church tower and ran off, earning himself the nickname of Captain Church.)

**Beaupre Castle,** *St. Hilary, Glamorgan. 2 miles south-east of Cowbridge.*

After the erection in the 19th Century of a "New Beaupre" mansion just west of St. Hilary, Beaupre Castle has also become known as Old Beaupre, and to the Welsh it is Bewpyr. The name is derived from the old French "beau-repaire", meaning beautiful retreat—which says two things about the building. Firstly, it indeed has a picturesque setting—on a steep bank in a curve of the River Thaw; and secondly, it has always been a peaceful residence, and not a castle at all. But the ruins give it a castle-like appearance, the eighteen-foot medieval curtain wall once had castellations, it still has the remains of a substantial gatehouse, and its siting shows that some consideration was given to defence. So naming it Beaupre Castle was not such a flight of fancy as that shown by the owners of some other manor houses.

The earliest work on the site dates from the 13th Century, and was probably erected by the family which was to hold Beaupre until 1709—the Bassets, who were descended from the earliest

Norman settlers. Both Beaupre Castle and the Bassets seem to have escaped involvement of any sort in Owain Glyndwr's uprising, but in the middle of the 16th Century the medieval buildings were largely abandoned, and the buildings which constitute the present remains were begun. Of the earlier works, only the gatehouse complex and adjacent curtain survive (though some parts are probably incorporated in the farm buildings, which are not open to the public). The major part of the Elizabethan manor was begun in about 1586, and the magnificent inner porch was added in 1600. Beaupre saw its most notable period immediately thereafter, and in 1643 Sir Richard Basset, a faithful Royalist, was made High Sherriff. In 1645 Charles I appointed him governor of

Cardiff Castle, but he was unpopular and was forced to abandon this post. On a journey to Hereford to surrender his commission to the King, Sir Richard was captured when the city fell to the Parliamentarian forces under Colonel Birch. He was fined £753, and this was the final blow in a list of misfortunes which were doubtless the main reason for the abandonment and gradual decline of Beaupre Castle. Sir Richard's son William was nevertheless notable enough to be buried at Westminster Abbey. The last Basset to live at Beaupre was the eldest son of William's half-brother, and after that the property changed hands a number of times. It is now in the care of the Department of the Environment.

By far the most striking feature of Beaupre Castle is the inner porch, and it is probably the finest of its kind in Wales. The extravagant sentiment of Elizabethan and Jacobean times is fully expressed, and although the architect is unknown, its design is similar in many ways to a series of splendid porches in Northamptonshire. The declining fortunes of Beaupre's inhabitants meant that none of the usual 18th Century embellishments were added, though in part of the farm there is some early 18th Century panelling.

**Benton Castle,** *Llangwm, Pembrokeshire. 6 miles east of Milford Haven.*

A fair amount of the structure of Benton Castle remains, and its original character is traceable, showing it to have been a very small enclosure castle with a round keep, and another round tower on the exposed side. The ward was polygonal, and the building dates from the late 13th Century. No contemporary history of the castle is known.

**Bleffda Castle,** *Bleffda, Radnorshire. 10 miles north-east of Llandrindod Wells on A488.*

Only the earthworks remain visible, but they show that a square tower stood on the motte, which was

*Opposite: striking aerial view of Beaumaris, the last of Edward I's great Welsh castles, which was begun in 1295*

mainly the natural formation of a ridge. The bailey was extremely small. Bleffda Castle was probably built late in the 12th Century—it is mentioned in the Pipe Roll of 1195 when building was in progress. It was attacked and captured in 1262, and recorded as being derelict in 1304.

**Boughrood Castle,** *Boughrood, Radnorshire. $8\frac{1}{2}$ miles north-east of Brecon, off B4350.*

A completely ruined castle which stood on a low motte. Although there is no sign of any bailey, recent excavations have revealed a considerable amount of fallen masonry in the motte, which indicates that originally the castle's main structure was a stone tower. Boughrood Castle was built in 1205, but this date is the only record of it that survives.

**Bovehill Castle,** *Cheriton, Glamorgan. 12 miles west of Swansea.*

Situated on Nottle Tor, a prominent limestone spar which overlooks an expanse of marshes, are the remains of extensive earthworks built by the Normans during their occupation of the Gower Peninsula at the end of the 11th Century.

**Brecon Castle,** *Brecon, Breconshire. In the grounds of Castle Hotel in town.*

A fortress was first built here at the end of the 11th Century by Bernard de Newmarch, a relative of William the Conqueror, and was a simple motte and bailey structure. De Newmarch had captured the kingdom of Brycheiniog from Welsh princes in 1094 and was granted numerous rights as Lord of Brecon in return. But the English tried repeatedly to expel him, and his fortification at Brecon showed his determination to hang on to his gains. A polygonal shell on the motte was added in the 12th Century, a hall and a round tower in the 13th Century, and a semi-octagonal tower early in the 14th Century.

Breconshire was frequently harassed by Owain Glyndwr during his rising in the early years of Henry IV's reign, and Sir Thomas Berkeley was at that stage put in charge of the castle. In 1404 the Lords of Audley and Warwick were appointed to defend Brecon, and were given 100 men-at-arms and 11 mounted archers. The castle had an eventful military life—its situation is a commanding one and possession of it was greatly sought after. It is recorded as being captured in 1215; attacked in 1231 and 1233; captured in 1264 and again in 1265; attacked in 1273, and again in 1403 by Owain Glyndwr's followers. A more peaceful event that took place in the castle was the projection of a marriage between Henry Tudor and Elizabeth, daughter of Edward IV, and the union of the Houses of York and Lancaster.

The walls of the 11th Century fortress were partly built of stones from the old Roman station of Caer Bannan, three miles away, which was the Welsh capital of Brycheiniog. Now the castle is much ruined, the chief remains being the structure on the motte known as Ely Tower, which was the prison of Morton, Bishop of Ely, in the reign of Richard III (1483–85), when a Duke of Buckingham was Lord of Brecon.

*Beaupre Castle, illustrating the magnificent inner porch designed by an unknown architect and added to the Elizabethan mansion in 1600*

**Bronllys Castle,** *Bronllys, Breconshire. 7½ miles north-east of Brecon on A479.*

This was a small castle, and probably a knight's stronghold, of which there were many in the 13th and 14th Centuries. The keep was a circular tower, now much ruined, which stood on an earlier Norman motte. The castle had two baileys, the main one being walled, and a small domestic block was probably added in the 16th Century. Accommodation in this type of castle was limited, but here a nearby church with detached tower would have provided additional shelter for women and children, and for livestock. The fortress was first documented in 1175, and is mentioned as being captured in local rebellions in 1233 and 1322.

*Brecon Castle—a view of rolling hills from a castle attacked six times, and captured three times, in the 13th Century alone*

grounds. There is, however, no record of any castle ever occupying the site, and nothing is known of the burial. (See Knighton Castle.)

**Bryn-y-Castell,** *Mold, Flintshire. 2½ miles south-east of Mold.*

Until fairly recently it was thought that this "Castle Hill" was the defensive mound of an early Welsh castle, but investigations have revealed that it could not possibly be a castle site. It is almost certainly a natural mound of moraine gravel, the debris left by a melting glacier at the end of the last Ice Age.

**Bryn Bras Castle,** *Llanrug, Caernarvonshire. 4 miles east of Caernarvon, off A4086.*

A comparatively modern mansion, built in 1830 around an earlier structure, Bryn Bras is best known for its extensive gardens which offer pleasant walks and impressive panoramic views of Anglesey and of Snowdonia. A few rooms in the buildings are also open, there are picnic areas in the gardens, fresh bread and scones from a neighbouring bakehouse, and a free car park.

**Builth Castle,** *Builth Wells, Breconshire. At the east end of the town.*

Little more than the earthworks and foundations now remain of a castle that was once one of considerable importance, being one of the eight castles built by Edward I to enforce his control over the Welsh. Builth Castle is even more ruined than Aberystwyth Castle, and it is difficult to realise that it was a companion to Flint and Rhuddlan, and a predecessor of Caernarvon,

**Bryn-y-Castell,** *Knighton, Radnorshire. In town recreation grounds on east side.*

Bryn-y-Castell is the name given long ago to this tumulus, or ancient burial mound, in the public

Conway, Harlech and Beaumaris Castles.
A castle occupied this site as early as 1168, when the capture of a castle here was recorded. It was rebuilt in 1219 and suffered an attack in 1223. In 1260, when it was being held for the English crown by Sir Roger Mortimer, it was captured and destroyed by the Welsh but retaken not long after. Edward I set in progress the complete rebuilding of the castle in 1277, the same year that Aberystwyth, Flint and Rhuddlan were begun. It is the scanty remains of this castle that can be seen today.

Edward's forces next invaded Wales in 1282, to try again to subdue the Welsh, who, led by Llywelyn, Prince of Wales, and his brother Dafydd, were restive under the harsh terms of the Treaty of Rhuddlan. Llywelyn moved south to his nearby retreat at Aberedw. With the English forces close in pursuit, Llywelyn tried to persuade the Builth garrison to support him, but was refused and met his death not far from the castle (see Aberedw Castle).

The fortification consisted of a round keep on a substantial motte, and two baileys formed by dividing the original large bailey. The motte tower was surrounded by masonry chemise work, and the main bailey had some stone defences; but much of the strength of the castle lay in its powerful earthworks which were mainly formed by a wet moat and a strong counterscarp bank which encircled the whole site.

# C

**Caergwrle Castle,** *Caergwrle, Flintshire. 6 miles south-east of Mold on A541.*

The few remnants of Caergwrle Castle show that it was a fairly small castle with three half-round towers and a small polygonal turret. It was set in a corner of a large earthwork enclosure which was possibly an earlier hill fort. Documents record that the castle was captured, destroyed and rebuilt in 1282, but no earlier or later history is traceable.

**Caerleon Castle,** *Caerleon, Monmouthshire. In town 3 miles north-east of Newport on A449.*

Caerleon saw centuries of Christian and Roman settlement and fortification before Norman invaders used this site for the steep motte of their castle in 1085. The motte had a tower, a two-towered barbican at the bottom, and the strong bailey eventually had at least a further two towers. The one tower that survives was probably erected in the middle of the 13th Century. The castle was attacked and captured in 1217, and resisted another attack by the Welsh in 1231.

The ancient and varied history of Caerleon has given rise to many legends, and it is often mentioned as being (as are other sites) the place where Arthur's palace stood, and from whose battlements it was possible (despite the intervening hills) to see the Bristol Channel. The castle enclosure is now surrounded by walls and the site is well wooded.

*Opposite: Bronllys Castle, Breconshire—*
*a simple round tower, typical of the small*
*strongholds maintained by obscure knights*
*in the 13th and 14th Centuries*

**Caernarvon Castle,** *Caernarvon, Caernarvonshire.
In town, at mouth of River Seiont.*

The Welsh castles of Edward I, especially the last
four, became renowned throughout Europe as
masterpieces of military architecture and engineering. They were immensely strong, using every
refinement of defence evolved in England, Europe
and even the Middle East during years of siege and
warfare. Yet while they look every bit as powerful as
they once were, they have also acquired, centuries
after the oppression they represented, a striking
and romantic beauty. Caernarvon Castle, even
more than Conway, Harlech, and Beaumaris, has
an image of military might and royal splendour
which has given it a special place among the castles
of Wales.

Since the investiture of the Prince of Wales in 1969
it has become even more famous, thanks to the
enormous television and press coverage of that
colourful pageant. Yet, long before, legend combined with history to single out Caernarvon as a
"royal" castle, though royalty frequented many
other castles as often. Even before 1969, and
before Prince Edward's investiture in 1911, it was
firmly associated with the title "Prince of Wales".
In April 1868 another Prince of Wales was welcomed in Caernarvon Castle "on this the anniver-
sary of the birth within these walls of the first
Prince of Wales"—the first, that is, who was the
eldest son of a monarch of England as well as
Wales.

When he had managed to subdue most of Wales,
Edward I placated the Welsh nobility with the
promise that he would present to both nations a
prince born in Wales, and who could speak no
English. Tradition insists that when Queen Eleanor
gave birth to Edward's son (who became the tragic
Edward II), the king presented the infant Prince to
the people at Caernarvon, fulfilling his promise—
he was born on Welsh soil (though in an English
castle) and he could speak no English (though no
Welsh either).

How much of this is true is, unfortunately, not
known (see Rhuddlan Castle). The same legend
insists that the birth-place was a small room in the
Eagle Tower (the most striking of the many towers
of Caernarvon Castle), yet records show that the
tower was not nearly complete in April 1284 when

the Prince was born. The story only seems to have
become widespread in Elizabethan times, and it is
also true that the young Edward was part of a large
family and at that time not even heir to the throne.
Since the first investiture of 1301, however, the
title "Prince of Wales" has usually been accorded
to the sovereign's eldest son, though it is conferred
by letters patent, and is not an automatic inheritance.

Caernarvon Castle's superb construction must
take as much credit for its enduring fame as the
legend which clings to it. Even Dr. Johnson spoke
of it as "an edifice of stupendous majesty and
strength". The principal designer was James of
St. George, Master of the King's Works in Wales,
a former mason whose genius can be traced in at
least six of Edward's Welsh castles, and in many
military structures in England as well. James of
St. George's "partner", Walter of Hereford, must
take credit as well, for although another legend
swears that the castle was built in a year, building
in fact went on for forty years—and even then the
castle was never finished. Walter took charge in
1294, eleven years after construction started, and
after his death in 1309, Henry of Ellerton became
Master of Works at Caernarvon. "Architects",
engineers, masons, and other craftsmen were
recruited from all over England, and from many
European countries as well; and when work
became more urgent after attacks and sieges,
press-gang methods were used to gather the necessary labourers. The castle was of course only part
of the defence on this strategic point designed to
keep the Welsh leaders in Anglesey. The town
walls and gates and the fortified quay were also
being built, and the whole defensive construction
for the town cost then about £19,000—in today's
terms over £2 million, making it the second
most expensive Edwardian project in Wales, only
Conway costing more.

The castle is built on the peninsula formed by the
mouth of the River Seiont and the Menai Strait,
and occupies the site of an earlier motte and bailey
castle built by the Norman Hugh de Lupus, Earl of
Chester, who took part in William the Conqueror's
invasion of 1066. The substantial motte influenced
the design, and has given the castle its familiar
"hour-glass" plan. The end of Henry I's reign
saw England plunged into anarchy and civil war,

and Owen Gwynedd rose in the north and won back much of the land previously lost. The next major conquest was by Edward I in 1277, when he built the castles of Flint, Rhuddlan, Aberystwyth and Builth. The treaty of Rhuddlan in 1277 stripped the Welsh of most of their rights and territories, and inevitably war broke out again, causing Edward's second invasion of 1282. Open warfare ended early in 1283 after the death of Llywelyn (see Aberedw Castle), and the capture and execution of his even more rebellious brother Dafydd, who was hung, drawn and quartered at Shrewsbury.

To enforce his conquest and protect the English settlers, the castles of Caernarvon, Conway and Harlech were then begun, and in 1295 work started on Beaumaris Castle. For proper protection a complete defensive structure had to be built simultaneously, and the castle, town walls and quay were all started, much of the material coming by water from Anglesey and from Chester and the nearby Roman legionary fort of Segontium.

By 1292 the whole external southern facade, from the massive Eagle Tower to the North East Tower, was up to a good height, and the town walls enclosed the settlers. In the summer of 1283, however, Edward and Queen Eleanor had only temporary accommodation during their visit, though decent masonry lodgings were available the following spring when Edward II was born. Most of the major structural work was in fact completed by 1287, work after that date mainly consisting of

*Caernarvon Castle, firmly associated with the first English Prince of Wales by legend if not by verifiable history.*

detailed finishing. The first governor, John de Havering, was appointed, and secure permanency seemed assured.

A shock came in 1294 when the Welsh prince Madoc raised a revolt, lynched the Sheriff of Caernarvon, and massacred many townspeople. Using the noisy festivities of a fair as cover, Madoc's supporters managed to work their way into the moat below the Eagle Tower where the castle wall was not completed. They seized the castle and set fire to much of the timber-work before being routed. Immediately Edward ordered a start on the defences on the north, or town side of the castle, this apparently being as vulnerable as the sides facing water. The north end between the town walls, with its towers and the King's Gate, were built from 1295 to 1301. More large-scale work went on in 1304 and 1305, and the last long building period lasted from 1309 to 1327.

By that time, however, Edward's descendants were firmly established as rulers and Wales was relatively peaceful. The castle became neglected, and only sixty years after it was begun Caernarvon Castle was in a bad state. Its iron, lead and glass were constantly pillaged, and eventually it was serving only as prison for comparatively minor offenders. When Richard II visited Caernarvon in 1399, while trying to decide on a course of action over his cousin Henry's demands, the castle could only offer him a bed of straw on the floor for a number of nights.

The castle's military purpose was revived in 1401 when Owain Glyndwr, aided by French soldiers, staged his desperate revolt and attacked and besieged Caernarvon—vainly, however, and with the loss of nearly 300 men. Glyndwr tried again in 1403, briefly, and the next year returned once more, this time armed with all the latest developments in siege equipment. But the castle's architects were even greater experts than the designers of the siege machines, and a garrison of only twenty-eight men was able to repel the Welsh assault.

The next period of calm was reinforced by the arrival on the throne of England of the Tudors, with their Welsh heritage, and this calm lasted to the time of Charles I. Caernarvon Castle then achieved some notoriety as the prison of the malicious Roundhead William Pryne, imprisoned for his attack in pamphlets on Archbishop Laud. The Star Chamber sentenced him to imprisonment for life, a fine of £500, to be branded on both cheeks with an "S" and an "L" (for seditious libeller), and to lose the "remainder" of his ears! His Puritan friends were incensed by the severity of the sentence, and flocked to Caernarvon in such large numbers that Pryne was moved to a castle on the island of Jersey.

Caernarvon Castle's final military chapter opened with the outbreak of the Civil War in 1642, when it was garrisoned for Charles I and the Royalists. In 1644 it was taken by a Parliamentarian force under Captain Sweeney. The next year the Royalists led by Lord Byron retook the castle, but lost it again in 1646 to the Parliamentarians under Major-General Mytton. Sir John Owen briefly and unsuccessfully besieged the castle before the first stage of the Civil War ended in Charles' surrender. After the Restoration, Charles II ordered the castle's destruction, but for some reason the order was never carried out. In the 20th century repairs and restoration were begun, the Government taking responsibility in 1908. Many improvements were made for the investitures of 1911 and 1969. From the outside the castle has withstood time and warfare well, and it is only from the inside that it is obviously a ruin. The external appearance, with its familiar dark bands of sandstone in lighter limestone, must be much the same now as in the 14th Century.

To all but the most determined besiegers, the sight of the castle must have been discouraging. The walls, seven to nine feet thick, were fortified by thirteen towers—pentagonal, octagonal and hexagonal. The only entrance now—there was a smaller second entrance, and a postern—is the beautiful and lofty archway of King's Gate, above which is a much worn statue of Edward II (a dozen iron spikes once discouraged birds from using this royal perch). Apart from the two massive towers flanking the entrance, the gate was defended by a drawbridge, five doors, and six portcullises, as well as by arrow slits and machicolations. The old Norman motte inhibited the castle plan which, instead of the concentric patterns of Harlech and Beaumaris, was to have followed Conway's example of having a cross wall giving an upper and a lower ward, but this part of the structure was never finished. However, the omission hardly weakened Caernarvon Castle—the superabundance of arrow slits, battlements, protruding towers, covered walkways, portcullises etc., made it so powerful that in 1284 a garrison of forty was considered sufficient for its defence.

One of the Castle's most striking features is the Eagle Tower, built so strongly that it resembled a keep, with its own portcullis and postern. It has three very fine turrets, and after the tower was completed, a unique hexagonal turret was added in 1316. The early defenders used to place stone figures on the battlements at the top of the tower which, being 128 feet above the ground, frequently persuaded the Welsh that the defenders were considerably more numerous. The tower perhaps got its name from the eagles on the arms of William de Grandson, though at least one of the stone ornaments on the battlements represents an eagle. The main room on the ground floor houses the laid-up colours of the Royal Welch Fusiliers, and the small room in which legend says Edward I was born can be visited. The normal entrance to the tower was from the courtyard into the ground floor, but there was also an entrance from the moat into the basement. The walls here are up to eighteen feet thick, and the only natural light is through a long narrow slit in the south wall.

The regimental museum of the Royal Welch Fusiliers is in the Queen Tower, the next tower south of Eagle Tower. Here a door close to the curtain wall gives access to a passage which leads to a corridor in the thickness of the wall, from which windows opened into the Banqueting Hall, originally 100 feet long, 45 feet wide and 50 feet high, though now only the outer wall remains.

The corridor leads on in the wall to Chamberlain Tower, through Black Tower and Cistern Tower to Queen's Gate. In Chamberlain Tower is the robing room used by the Prince of Wales before the investiture of 1969, and preserved as it was then. Black Tower contains the smallest rooms in the castle, and it was probably always used as a prison. Cistern Tower still has its old stone tank, and Queen's Gate beyond it was the original entrance to the castle before the extra defences of 1295–1301 were built. North of Queen's Gate, and completing the short eastern side of the "hour-glass", is the North-East Tower (Eagle Tower is at

the north-west angle) in which an investiture exhibition can be seen. The last big tower before King's Gate's eastern tower is reached is the Granary Tower. Much of the castle's covered wall walks, galleries and wall passages can still be used, and in the small Watch Tower between Queen's Gate and North-East Tower, grooves can be seen where shutters were hung to protect archers.

**Caerphilly Castle,** *Caerphilly, Glamorgan. In town, 9 miles north of Cardiff.*

These are the remains of the largest castle in Wales, covering some 30 acres, and the first concentric castle in Britain. Caerphilly Castle was also one of the finest examples of the power possible by a combination of land and water defences. It was remarkably well guarded against surprise attacks, with three distinct wards and seven strong gatehouses in the castle itself and in the outer curtain wall, which formed a large and powerful barbican. The inner bailey is roughly square, with four large towers and two substantial gatehouses. Each tower and each gatehouse was isolated from both the court and the walls by regular portcullised doorways, giving thirty portcullises in all. The lower work around the castle was protected by lakes and a fortified dam, with revetted outwork on the other side. Although the castle's designer is unknown, the high standard of its military engineering and design, and its many similarities with the later concentric castles of Harlech and Beaumaris castles suggest that James of St. George had some part to play.

Nor are many details known of Caerphilly Castle's history, though it is known that it was begun in 1268 by Gilbert de Clare, Earl of Gloucester and Lord of Glamorgan, as a stronghold against Llywelyn, Prince of Wales, who had extended his influence as far south as Glamorgan's northern borders. Gilbert de Clare's site for his first castle was close to earlier fortifications put up by the Romans about A.D. 75, now hidden beneath the North-West Earthwork. After the Romans left, the area remained in Welsh hands even through the Norman conquest of Glamorgan in 1090, and a Welsh castle mound is also obscured within the North-West Earthwork. The castle of 1268, covering the main route to Cardiff, was unsuccessful, and soon after work was begun Llywelyn invaded the district and destroyed all that had been built.

Earl Gilbert began the present castle in 1271 on the same site as his previous one, and once again before it was finished, Llywelyn attacked. Attempting to reconcile the opponents, Henry III intervened and work on the castle stopped while it was made neutral territory. But before any agreement could be reached Gilbert took possession of the castle by force, and faced with a unity of barons on the Earl's side, Llywelyn withdrew.

Caerphilly Castle took no part in the struggles of Edward I's Welsh wars of 1277 and 1282, and with the subjugation of united Welsh power by 1283 such a powerful fortress at Caerphilly was not necessary, though it was a useful strongpoint from which the district could be governed, taxes collected, and courts held. Through much of Wales there was still sporadic unrest, with local chieftains staging brief, violent, but usually unsuccessful revolts. That led by Llywelyn Bren of Gelligaer, five miles to the north of Caerphilly, resulted in widespread destruction through Glamorgan, and it took combined attacks from the directions of Cardiff and Brecon to end the revolt. Caerphilly Castle, attacked and besieged, saw out the unrest safe in English hands.

It was not long before the castle again attracted attention, this time on a grander scale. Earl Gilbert's daughter had married Hugh le Despenser, Edward II's influential and unpopular favourite, and he had succeeded his father-in-law as Lord of Glamorgan. Despenser's unpopularity increased among his neighbouring barons as he used his influence on Edward to increase his territories, and in 1321 the barons united, attacked Glamorgan, and captured Caerphilly Castle. But his king came to Despenser's rescue—he led his army into Wales, subdued the revolt, and reinstated his favourite.

The king's unhappy reign was nearing its end, however, for in 1326 Queen Isabella landed in East Anglia with the band of exiled nobles she had gathered during her negotiations in France, ostensibly on Edward II's behalf. The king immediately fled to Wales and his companion in Caerphilly Castle, making it his temporary headquarters. Soon he fled further west to Neath, heading for Ireland in such a panic that much of his treasure was forgotten in the castle. The Queen's army was not far behind, and besieged Caerphilly in the winter of 1326–27. It was a long and bitter siege, countered by an able defence using all of the castle's formidable power, and continued until April, though Edward was captured near Llantrisant in November and his son, Prince Edward, was proclaimed king in January. Even in April, the castle only surrendered when a favourable peace settlement was offered. The final chapters of this era in the castle's history were as tragic as the earlier ones—the Despensers were beheaded at Bristol not long after, and in September Edward was horribly murdered at Berkeley Castle. It is not surprising that the local Welsh looked with dread on the castle's massive fortifications, and one Bard's poem expresses the wish that an enemy's soul "may go to Caerphilly".

The castle's last major military event was its brief capture by Owain Glyndwr during his revolt at the beginning of the 15th Century, but after that it fell into neglect; by 1536 it was in decay, Leland describing it as a wilderness of ruinous walls. In the Civil War of 1642 the Royalists greatly increased the North-West Earthwork to take artillery and defend the north approach, finally destroying and obscuring forever the last traces of the Roman fort. Exactly what happened at Caerphilly during and after the Civil War is not known, but most probably it was slighted under Cromwell's orders, and the lakes were drained.

Much restoration work was carried out by the 3rd and 4th Marquises of Bute, and houses and other buildings which clustered around its walls were cleared away. World War II intervened, the Government taking over guardianship of the castle in 1949.

One of the most absorbing individual features of Caerphilly Castle is its leaning tower, a massive piece of masonry 50 feet high and at least nine feet out of perpendicular, rivalling leaning towers anywhere. Accounts vary as to how it got into this striking position. The most romantic, but also most unlikely account is that during Queen Isabella's siege of 1326–27 the besiegers made a determined attack on this tower, from which molten lead was being poured on them. They managed to penetrate the tower and make their way to the furnaces and melting pots, and then, either by design or through ignorance, opened the moat into the furnace room, causing an explosion of steam that blew out part of the foundations. But it is unlikely that such a leaning tower would have remained for so long without written comment, or that some attempt would not have been made to shore it up. (Historians also discount the popular idea of such a precious commodity as lead being used in this way.) The tower's crisis was

doubtless caused by an explosion of some sort, but it almost certainly happened during or shortly after the Civil War, either by an accidental explosion of gunpowder, or by an unsuccessful Parliamentarian attempt to slight the castle. Whatever caused the tower partially to collapse, it remains as an awesome curiosity, and a tribute to the workmanship of the masons who built it.

Apart from this single curiosity, Caerphilly Castle is best appreciated by regarding its total concept as a massive and extremely strong defensive structure, and a study of a plan of the whole site

shows how consideration was given to defence against all the methods of attack and siege machines then known. Even the normally sufficient concentric castle pattern at Caerphilly forms only a part of the elaborate plan of land and water defences that make it unique.

**Caldicot Castle,** *Caldicot, Monmouthshire. In town, 4½ miles south-west of Chepstow on B4245.*

Caldicot Castle was a substantial Norman stronghold on the site of an earlier Saxon castle built in the early 12th Century. The Norman round keep on the large motte was built in the early 13th Century, and the outer wall had four round towers, one forming a curious gate. The baronial hall was added about 100 years later, and the two gates nearly a century after that. The castle's history is obscure, but it did once belong to the Duchy of Lancaster.

**Camlais Castle**—see Cwm Camlais Castle.

**Candleston Castle**, *Merthyrmawr, Glamorgan. 3 miles south-west of Bridgend.*

The ruins of Candleston Castle are a mixture of a square tower and polygonal courtyard dating from the 14th Century, and fortified domestic buildings a hundred years younger. The mansion was once owned by a branch of the powerful Cantelupe family, and was inhabited up to Victorian times. Now, however, it is in complete decay and the lands to the south have been overwhelmed by the shifting sand dunes.

**Cardiff Castle**, *Cardiff, Glamorgan. In Castle Street, west of city centre.*

On a site that has seen constant occupation from Roman times until 1947, evidence can also be seen of building covering as great a span—Roman walls, a 12th Century keep, medieval apartments, and 19th Century rooms and reconstruction.

Cardiff Castle was built by Robert FitzHamon, perhaps on the site of the smaller Welsh fortress of the princes of Morganwy, and was probably started in 1081. The keep was built later on a motte 40 feet high situated in the north-west corner of the Roman camp, the motte being surrounded by a moat. Soon after the keep was built it became the prison of Robert, Duke of Normandy, brother of William Rufus and Henry I. He was imprisoned by Henry after the latter captured Bayeaux and Caen—Robert's last strongholds—and after his decisive victory over Robert at Tinchebrai in 1106. Robert died in the castle, 28 years later, having had a truly miserable imprisonment, for from the first his eyes had been put out "for greater security".

Nearly 25 years after the Duke of Normandy's death, the Welsh made a successful attack on Cardiff Castle. Although it was well garrisoned, and

the town was full of the castle lord's paid retainers, the Welsh took possession and abducted the Earl of Gloucester, the Countess and their only son. Only by granting the Welsh valuable concessions were the English able to save the Gloucesters.

In the 13th Century the castle was strengthened by the construction of the Black Tower and various walls which had to be passed before an attack on the keep could be made. The Black Tower has an apt name—in it is an unlit, unventilated dungeon which can only be entered through a trap door in the floor of the chamber above it. This gruesome room no doubt gave rise to the belief that the tower was the Duke of Normandy's prison, but there is no doubt that it was built long after his death.

In 1404, during the reign of Henry IV, Owain Glyndwr caused much destruction to the town and part of the castle defences in the later stages of his uprising. For further defence a great octagonal tower, still a significant feature of the Castle, was begun in 1425, as were a number of domestic buildings. Two hundred years later, in the Civil War, the castle was held for the Royalists and changed hands more than once, until the Royalists were defeated at St. Fagan's, about four miles from Cardiff.

Nothing more of significance seems to have happened to the Castle until the end of the 18th Century, when the north wing and the drawing room were added. Among other reconstruction and additions, the octagonal tower gained a spire in 1875.

The chief interior features (through which a guided tour can be taken) are mostly those belonging to the castle's later years. The upper parts of the windows in the Winter Smoking Room display Saxon gods, and the library is a magnificent room 75 feet long. In the Drawing Room is a Louis XVIII period clock invented by one of the castle's many owners, the 3rd Earl of Bute, who was then, briefly, Prime Minister to George III. One of the most notable older rooms is the Banqueting Hall. Originally constructed in the 15th Century, it is lined with walnut wainscoting above which are frescoes which depict incidents in the life of Robert, Earl of Gloucester, the 2nd Lord of Cardiff Castle, who was custodian of the Duke of Normandy. Other noteworthy rooms are the Chaucer Room reached by a stairway in the thickness of the wall of the great octagonal tower, and the private chapel with its marble lining ornamented with enamelled shields, and its sacred illustrations on the walls and ceilings.

## Cardigan Castle, *Cardigan, Cardiganshire. In town.*

The early history of Cardigan Castle (at Nat. Grid Ref. SN 177459) is much confused with the history of Cardigan Old Castle (at SN 164464). It is likely that a castle was founded on this site in 1160 by Gilbert de Clare, though some sources say the first castle was a Welsh one built by Rhys ap Gruffydd. He certainly held it at some stage, and entertained several hundred people at the castle at Christmas 1177, at the festival of the Welsh bards. Whoever first built the castle, it was frequently wrecked and captured, restored and captured again, for it was on a much desired site on foreland overlooking the Teifi.

The remains of a circular keep and part of the perimeter, with two towers, probably date from the major rebuilding (in stone) and additional fortifications of about 1240, and later Edward I seems to have stayed in Cardigan Castle for about a month while settling the affairs of south-west Wales. In the Civil War of the 17th Century the castle was at first held by the Royalists, but when the Parliamentarians took possession they wrecked it to make it useless as a stronghold.

## Cardigan Old Castle, *Cardigan, Cardiganshire. 1 mile south-west of Cardigan.*

Hardly anything remains of the first castle set up in this vicinity. It was built in 1093, probably by Roger of Montgomery, who held it as fief for William Rufus. It was also the home of Cadwgan, a Welsh prince of Powys, who played a prominent part in the defence of Wales against the Norman invaders. The castle was destroyed in 1165 and rebuilt in stone in 1171. The records of a castle in this area being captured five times between 1198 and 1231 refer either to this castle or to Cardigan Castle in the town, but the more recent references, though few, must refer to the newer castle.

## Carew Castle, *Carew, Pembrokeshire. 4 miles east of Pembroke off A4075.*

It is doubtful whether any of the fine ruins which can be seen now date back to the earliest castle which was on the territory of Rhys, Prince of South Wales, and which, in 1095, passed into the hands of the Norman Gerald de Windsor when he married Nest, daughter of the Prince. The earliest remains are probably the blocked gate—either late 12th Century or early 13th Century—and the ruins of four large towers built about 100 years later.

The castle's original character was considerably changed in Tudor times. In the 15th Century a descendant of Gerald and Nest, Sir Edmund Carew, mortgaged the castle to Sir Rhys ap Thomas, the chief Welsh supporter of Henry VII, who stayed at Carew as Rhys's guest on the march to Bosworth Field and victory over Richard III. Sir Rhys partly rebuilt Carew Castle, and added sumptuous state apartments in keeping with his lavish and exuberant habits. Equally in keeping were the celebrations he gave on St. George's Day 1507, to celebrate being made a Knight of the Garter. The festivities lasted a week, were attended by over 600 nobles from all over south-west Wales, and included an apparently extremely successful tournament.

Many more domestic building changes and additions were made later by another wealthy owner, Sir John Perrott—whose father, it was reputed, was Henry VIII. After this period the castle's story seems to have been peaceful and obscure. Its whole military history was curiously uneventful, and even in the Civil War of 1642 it suffered little, surrendering after a brief siege (and after the fall of nearby Tenby Castle) to Cromwell's men. The ruins have revealed secret passages and dungeons.

small round tower from the 14th Century.

Carmarthen has a long history—it was the Roman settlement of Moridunum, and in the Dark Ages was "Merlin's City", the wizard and enchanter having apparently been born nearby. Later, when the castle was the principal residence of the princes of South Wales, it was frequently attacked by the English—and by the Welsh themselves, when they were trying to recover it from the invaders. Owain Glyndwr captured the castle in 1403, when his revolt was in full swing, lost it, and retook it again with French support in 1405.

**Carmarthen Castle,** *Carmarthen, Carmarthenshire. In town.*

Two towers, the gatehouse and the outer walls of Carmarthen Castle remain intact, but they are greatly obscured by more recent buildings and cannot be seen clearly from the town side. The castle was a strong motte and bailey defence, with the motte revetted for part of its height. It was first built in either 1094 or 1105, destroyed in 1215, and then rebuilt powerfully in stone in 1223. The towers date from that period, the gatehouse and a

In the Civil War of 1642–46 Carmarthen Castle changed hands more than once. Like most Welsh castles it was initially held by the Royalists, who threw up the earthworks called the Bulwarks, which can still be seen to the west of the town. The victorious Parliamentarians eventually dismantled most of the castle. It is now owned by the Local Authority.

**Carreg Cennen Castle,** *Trapp, Carmarthenshire. 3 miles south-east of Llandeilo.*

Carreg Cennen Castle offers one of the most striking sights in Wales. In the foothills of the awesome Black Mountains, the ruined fortress stands on a massive rock, and on three sides precipitous crags plunge 300 feet to the valley of the Afon Cennen. On the only accessible side two towers command the long, slowly rising ridge, while on the other sides the walls of the castle continue the sheer rise of the rock face.

Carreg Cennen was the centre of the ancient commote of Is-Cennen, part of the Welsh kingdom of Deheubarth (south-west Wales) which had its royal seat at Dynevor near Llandeilo. The Normans organised the commotes into lordships from their castles at Cardigan, Pembroke and Carmarthen, but while there was a Welsh castle resisting the Normans at Llandovery in 1116, there is no record of any castle at Carreg Cennen. Yet there must have been one there by that date—the nearby township was called Trecastell, and finds on the castle site indicate that it might once have held a Roman hill fort.

The Dynevor territories were inherited by Rhys ap Gruffydd, the Lord Rhys (1135–1197), and largely as a result of his determined resistance Deheubarth had its independence recognised by Henry II. In those times few inheritances went unchallenged or without bitterness, and that following Lord Rhys's death was no exception. Eventually Rhys Fychan inherited Carreg Cennen with Dynevor—and had to face the opposition of his uncle Maredudd at Dryslwyn, and even that of his Norman mother. Her hatred for her son resulted in the castle's first documented record; in 1248 it was mentioned that Rhys had won back his castle after his mother had

deceitfully passed it into English hands. Rhys also managed to drive out Maredudd, who then joined up with Llywelyn, Prince of Wales; together they returned and ejected Rhys, Maredudd taking over Rhys's territories in 1257.

Llywelyn's success in uniting minor Welsh leaders and princes in the north was not entirely repeated in the south-west, however, and in 1277 Edward's forces met little opposition as they advanced up the Towy from Kidwelly. Carreg Cennen Castle fell to the English, though the Welsh held it again briefly during Edward's second campaign in 1282. After the war the castle stayed in English care—specifically that of John Giffard, who was also in charge of Llandovery Castle. Giffard began extensive rebuilding, but the Welsh captured the castle during Rhys ap Maredudd's rising in 1286, and the Earl of Hereford took custody for a while after the Welsh surrendered. Giffard returned, and held Carreg Cennen for sixteen years altogether, being succeeded by his son. Most of the existing buildings were put up by the Giffards, and the earlier appearance of the castle was lost forever.

During the control of Giffard the younger, Edward II came to the throne and the hated royal favourite, Hugh le Despenser, became the most powerful baron in South Wales as he acquired power and territories by marriage and by his influence over the weak king. When Despenser tried to take over Gower as well, in 1321, a coalition of Marcher Lords, including Giffard, opposed him. After only a brief concession to the barons, Edward sent in his forces, defeated the coalition, and heaped new territories on Despenser. Among the grants Despenser received was Carreg Cennen Castle, and among the barons executed for rebellion was Giffard.

After Despenser's execution by Queen Isabella's followers four years later the castle changed hands frequently, and in 1340 Edward III had it granted to Henry of Lancaster, Lord of Kidwelly, who later became Duke of Lancaster. John of Gaunt married the Lancaster heiress, and so he acquired Carreg Cennen in 1362, passing it on his death to his heir, Henry Bolingbroke. On his accession as Henry IV, it became Crown property as part of the Duchy of Lancaster.

Carreg Cennen's formidable defences were attacked by Owain Glyndwr during the second year of his rebellion, in 1403. Whether or not he actually managed to capture the castle is uncertain. He held much of Wales, and had taken many towns, but some sources say that Carreg Cennen (which could only be taken by vicious sudden attack or a long siege) proved too much for him, even after he tried both methods. Nevertheless there is a 1416 record of repairs to all the stone walls of the castle which had been "completely destroyed and thrown down by rebels".

In the Wars of the Roses Carreg Cennen was held for the House of Lancaster, and was garrisoned and repaired by Gruffydd ap Nicholas when hostilities began in 1455. After the Yorkist victory at Mortimer's Cross, Gruffydd's sons Thomas and Owain took refuge in the castle. They were persuaded to surrender in 1462 by Sir Richard Herbert of Raglan, and a few months later it was decided to demolish the castle. Five hundred men, armed with picks and crowbars, slighted Carreg Cennen, and after that it was of little use.

Henry VII granted the castle to his supporter Sir Rhys ap Thomas, and it belonged to the Vaughans of Golden Grove from the 16th to early 19th Centuries. The Vaughan estates were bequeathed to the 1st Baron Cawdor, and Earl Cawdor and his ancestors did much to preserve the ruins, eventually placing the castle in the care of the Department of the Environment (then H.M. Office of Works) in 1932.

There is little documentary record of the construction of the present castle, but work seems to have been done over three main periods in the late 13th and early 14th Centuries. The earliest part is the towered inner ward, which forms the nucleus of the castle, with its fine gatehouse and chapel tower, and only sections of the west and south curtain walls indicate the castle's Welsh predecessor. After the inner ward, the barbican was constructed, and then the outer ward. Many repairs were made in 1369 (by which time the castle was in very poor condition), the work being carried out by Lancastrian officials from Kidwelly.

Approach to the castle was up a long ridge, through the walled outer ward, up the heavily guarded barbican ramp (which included a middle drawbridge), and then into the inner ward through the gatehouse, which was defended by a drawbridge, portcullis and door, and made into a potential isolated stronghold by another portcullis and door on its inner end.

Apart from its stirring setting, one of the castle's most interesting features is the long passage leading down through the south cliff face to a cave below the castle. For much of its length it was bored out of the rock, walled and vaulted, with light coming from apertures in the cliff face— these now offering breathtaking views of the valley below and of the Black Mountains. The cave, which runs about 50 yards into the hill, had its opening walled up to make its only access the passage from the castle. Although it seems to have been used as a dovecot, and has a spring, its incorporation into the castle was probably to prevent enemies occupying it and undermining the castle itself.

The setting of Carreg Cennen Castle is one that awakens the imagination, and it is not surprising to hear that there is a legend of mystery associated with the site. Many years ago a local farmer is said to have come across a seated, cloaked figure in the Castle Cave on the river bank. This figure is reputed to have been the immortal body of Owain Llawgoch (a hero of Wales and known to the French in the 14th Century as Owain of Wales) who, like Arthur, was waiting to be summoned to rescue his country from peril. Owain had been murdered by his traitorous servant while he led a French sponsored expedition to save Wales in the reign of Edward III—to the relief of Edward, and the mourning of Wales and France. There is perhaps more than coincidence in the Welsh rebellion less than a hundred years later, which was led by another Owain (Glyndwr), and strongly supported by the French.

**Castell Allt-goch,** *Lampeter, Cardiganshire. 1½ miles north-east of Lampeter.*

Not a castle at all, but a tumulus or ancient burial ground described by the historian Gerald de Barri as being close to the battlefield where, in 1134, Gruffydd, son of Rhys ap Tewdwr, defeated an English army. Local folklore says that the tumulus —a Celtic relic—will adapt itself to the shape of anyone who lies down to sleep on it. Weary knights and soldiers, however, will awaken refreshed but angry, for the mound also has the habit of breaking armour to pieces.

**Castell near Barmouth,** *Merioneth. On footpath 1½ miles north of Barmouth, within a bend of A496.*

Close to disused manganese workings, in a fine and prominent situation, is the ruin of an ancient hill fort.

**Castell-y-Bere,** *Llanfihangel-y-Pennant, Merioneth. 7 miles south-west of Dolgellan.*

Castell-y-Bere is one of the castles of Wales which has a special place in the country's history. It was once one of the largest, most important and carefully designed and constructed Welsh castles, and was probably begun by Llywelyn the Great in 1221. It also became one of the most richly ornamented of these castles, and saw a lot of the rulers of Wales in the alternately optimistic and despairing years before Edward I crushed so many hopes in 1277. After the Treaty of Rhuddlan in 1277, Dafydd, brother of Llywelyn, the last Prince of Wales, established himself in Castell-y-Bere, and, like many other Welsh leaders, grew restive under Edward's harsh terms. In 1282 Dafydd seized Hawarden, and once again there was warfare between Wales and Edward I.
But Edward was far too powerful, and before long Llywelyn was killed near Builth while trying to raise support from his castle at Aberedw. Castell-y-Bere became the last point of resistance to Edward, but eventually Dafydd had to take refuge in the mountains round Snowdon, and Castell-y-Bere surrendered to Edward. Dafydd was captured not long after—betrayed by some of his countrymen who believed his cause was hopeless—and went to a cruel death.

The ruins of the castle, overgrown with ivy, reveal an irregular plan on the rocky crest. All the work dates from the early 13th Century and the castle still shows the layout of the rectangular keep, three towers, and the large triangular barbican. It was destroyed by Edward in 1294 and mentioned only once again—as being in grave danger. It is now in the care of the Department of the Environment.

**Castell Blaen-llynfi,** *Bwlch, Breconshire. 7 miles east-south-east of Brecon off B4560.*

Little remains of this castle, but it is possible to trace its original structure to reveal a rounded ward, walled-in by masonry of a very inferior quality which has now almost entirely collapsed. There was an outer earthwork ward, and an earthwork dam provided wet defences. Almost nothing is known of the castle—it was captured in 1215, and was never mentioned again after 1322.

**Castell-y-blaidd,** *Llanbadarn Fynydd, Radnorshire. 7½ miles south of Newton.*

The site of an old castle, probably Welsh, with only scanty remains. It appears to have no documented history.

**Castell Carndochan,** *Llanuwchllyn, Merioneth. 11 miles north-east of Dolgellan.*

Little of Castell Carndochan's structure remains, but it was once a Welsh castle with a D-shaped keep. It is set on a lofty position along the course of the Afon Lliw, in an area once important to the Romans—nearby is a fort, and the ancient workings of a gold mine. Carndochan was probably built in the mid-13th Century, and it had an irregular ward with a round tower and a semi-circular tower. Its history is unknown.

**Castell Cawr,** *Abergele, Denbighshire. 1 mile south-east of Abergele.*

Castell Cawr is now no more than a tree-covered hill on which once stood a Roman fort. There are pleasant views into the Vale of Clwyd from the hill top.

**Castell Coch,** *Ystradfellte, Breconshire. 11 miles south-west of Brecon.*

On a sharp ridge are the featureless fragments of a small walled fortification. The castle is mentioned in documents in 1230, and it perhaps had a round tower or a keep, and a large hall room.

**Castell Coch,** *Tongwynlais, Glamorgan. 5 miles north-west of Cardiff on A470.*

The colour of its stone also makes Castell Coch known under its English translation of "Red Castle", and as long ago as 1307 it was referred to in documents as *Rubeum Castrum*. It was originally a fairly small Welsh castle on a large, low motte. The plan was roughly triangular, with a round tower at each of the three angles. The curtain wall was slightly curved on the longest side opposite the three towers, and had numerous arrow slits. Construction was started in about 1260, and probably went on until the early 14th Century.

*Castell-y-Bere, begun by Llywelyn the Great in 1221, and Dafydd's last stronghold in his vain rebellion sixty years later*

Castell Coch fell into disuse and was deliberately destroyed sometime in the 15th Century. It lay as a ruin until 1870, when William Burgess designed and carried out the almost complete rebuilding of the castle as a "folly" for the 3rd Marquess of Bute. The exterior is a painstaking and successful attempt to reproduce a medieval castle on its original foundations, and it is picturesquely situated in a thickly wooded height, in an area that has much natural beauty. The castle is now in the care of the Department of the Environment, and its interior is a striking example of unrestrained Victorian decoration.

**Castell Coch,** *Marletwy, Pembrokeshire. 7½ miles east of Haverfordwest.*

This Castell Coch was really only a strong house, and the hall block had only slight pretensions as a defensive structure. It was probably built in the 15th Century, but was later surrounded by a very strong earthwork ditch. There is no known history of the place, which is adjacent to the large Canaston Wood, but much of its structure remains.

**Castell Collen,** *Llanyre, Radnorshire. 1 mile north of Llandrindod Wells.*

Castell Collen (Castle of the Hazel Tree) is the site of an old Roman fort, which was possibly the one once known as Magos. The stone walls were eight feet thick, and the buildings within the walls were also of stone. Finds made during excavations are in the county museum in Llandrindod Wells.

*Opposite: Castell Coch, Glamorgan: a medieval castle site imaginatively restored in the 1870s, on a wooded hilltop of striking beauty*

**Castell Crugerydd,** *Llanfihangel Nant Melan, Radnorshire. 6 miles east of Llandrindod Wells.*

The scanty remains of an old Welsh castle, mentioned only once in history, in 1188, and that of no significance.

**Castell Crychydd,** *Clydey, Pembrokeshire. 8½ miles south-west of Cardigan.*

These fragmentary ruins are all that remain of a small castle, also sometimes known as Heron's Castle. It consisted of a defensive ringwork, made up of a wall of stone slabs laid in clay, and a bailey. The castle seems to have no recorded history.

**Castell Cwm Aran,** *Llandewi Ystradenny, Radnorshire. 8 miles north-east of Llandrindod Wells.*

Almost all trace of this early Norman castle has vanished. It was first documented as being rebuilt in 1144, was repaired in 1179 and rebuilt once more in 1195, which is the last heard of it.

**Castell Ddinas,** *Genffordd, Breconshire. 8½ miles east of Brecon, off A479.*

Little of the structure of Castell Ddinas remains, but it is possible to trace the arrangements of what was a fairly large castle when it was built, probably in the 12th Century. The castle's inner ward, with its small rectangular towers apparently divided into two, was set up inside an ancient hill fort. Some kind of chemise was drawn around the oblong keep. The castle was taken by the Welsh in 1233.

**Castell Dinas Bran,** *Llangollen, Denbighshire. On hill ½ mile north-east of Llangollen.*

The ruins of this rather mysterious, secluded 13th

Century castle top the detached and suddenly rising "Hill of Bran", and it is sometimes, but erroneously, called Crow Castle, "crow" being a possible meaning of "Bran". It was probably built by Gruffydd ap Madoc in about 1236, and consisted of a large square keep in a rectangular ward guarded by a twin-towered gatehouse and one large D-shaped tower. Near the main entrance is a room with three small circular holes in its vaulted roof—a curiosity which has long puzzled experts. Its architecture and construction, too, are curious, being neither traditional Norman nor Welsh.

The walls were chiefly built of small slaty stones set in mortar, and perhaps the fact that Gruffydd ap Madoc was a Welshman who took the side of Henry III against the Welsh had some influence on the castle's design, though most of the blame for the traitor's action should go to Gruffydd's English wife, for she weaned his sympathies. The Welsh made no such distinction, however, and Dinas Bran became Gruffydd's refuge with his furious countrymen. Gruffydd was the son of the founder of Vallé Crucis Abbey two miles to the north-east, and both he and his father are buried there.

A foundation of heaped rock on the site hints at a very early date for some settlement on the hill, and it is likely that the castle was preceded by a hill fort. Some accounts assert it was a stronghold of Eliseg, Prince of Powys in the 8th Century, while others use literary and legendary associations with various meanings of "Bran" to suggest the castle's descent from the 5th Century. Its end is as uncertain as its beginning—the last documented references are to its capture from the Welsh in 1277 and again in 1282—but there is a belief that it was besieged by Owain Glyndwr at the beginning of the 15th Century, when it was defended by Thomas

Fitzalan, Earl of Arundel. By the time of Henry VIII it was a ruin, and the historian Leland wrote of a fierce eagle that came to Dinas Bran every year to breed, and attacked anyone who approached its nest. The truth of that will doubtless never be known, but the underground passage rumoured to run between the castle and an advance post one mile to the west, might yet be found.

**Castell Dinas Emrys,** *Beddgelert, Caernarvonshire. 12 miles south-east of Caernarvon, off A498.*

Dinas Emrys was a Welsh castle, now badly ruined, most probably built at the beginning of the 13th Century. The square towered defence was built on a site whose great natural strength had been long appreciated, for it previously held a Dark Ages fort. There seems to be no record of the castle's history.

**Castell Dol-Wllf,** *Llanbyther, Cardiganshire. 4½ miles south-west of Lampeter on B4337.*

Another scattered ruin of a Welsh castle, about which nothing is known.

**Castell Dyffryn-mawr,** *Crymmych Arms, Pembrokeshire. 7 miles south of Cardigan.*

Only the earthworks remain of a small ringwork fortification whose stone slabs seemed to have been laid with clay, or a very poor mortar.

**Castell Du,** *Sennybridge, Breconshire. 8 miles west of Brecon, junction A40 and A4067.*

Castell Du (also known as Sennybridge Castle) is now much ruined. It was possibly a Welsh castle of the 13th Century which was never properly completed, and had a round tower attached to a

*Opposite: the ruins of mysterious Castell Dinas Bran, stronghold of the 13th Century Welsh turncoat Gruffyd ap Madoc, which has several curious and unexplained features*

small building block. The castle's history is unknown, and it was only mentioned once in documents, in 1271.

**Castell Fflemish,** *Tregaron, Cardiganshire. 2 miles north-west of Tregaron, off A485.*

Recent examinations have determined that this was not a castle, but an Iron Age site.

**Castell-y-Gaer,** *Llanegryn, Merioneth. 2½ miles north of Towyn.*

Another "castell" that was never a castle, but an ancient hill fort. The high point upon which it was sited gives an impressive view over Cardigan Bay.

**Castell Garn Fadryn,** *Garn, Caernarvonshire. 6 miles west of Pwllheli.*

Inside a great Iron-Age hill fort on Carn Fadryn are the completely ruined remains of a late 12th Century castle. Carn Fadryn means Madryn Mountain, and Madryn Castle is close by.

**Castell Goetre,** *Llanfair-Clydogau, Cardiganshire. 2½ miles north-east of Lampeter.*

The readiness to believe in legend, and the enthusiasm for naming almost any pile of rocks and mounds "castell", lay many false tracks for castle seekers. Castell Goetre is another misnomer—no castle seems to have stood here, but there are signs that the Romans mined silver and lead, and the church is set in a prehistoric oval-shaped earthwork.

**Castell Gwallter,** *Llandre, Cardiganshire. 4 miles north-east of Aberystwyth off B4353.*

Castell Gwallter was a small castle set on the escarpment, with a low motte and a rock-cut ditch. It was apparently destroyed in 1136, but it may have been repaired, and it is thought that it is perhaps the Pengwern Castle mentioned in documents of 1151.

**Castell Gwynionydd,** *Llandyssul, Cardiganshire. 12 miles west-south-west of Lampeter.*

Castell Gwynionydd seems to have no known history, but this is more than made up for by a legend associated with a curious and very large mound nearby, which has been variously attributed to the Iron Age, to Celts, Romans, Danes and Normans. Legend lays the responsibility elsewhere. The far-too-virtuous people of Pentre-cwrt across the Teifi were apparently a thorn in the side of the Devil who, with a gigantic spadeful of earth,

planned to dam the Teifi and drown them. But on his way he met a cobbler from Llandyssul carrying a sackful of shoes to be mended. They talked, and on learning the Devil's plan the cobbler pointed out that it was still a long way to Pentre-cwrt, and displayed his sack of broken shoes as evidence of how many he had worn out on this great distance. The Devil was taken in, did not think his plan was worth quite so much effort, and threw down his great spadeful of earth in disgust.

**Castell Hendre,** *Henry's Moat, Pembrokeshire. 8 miles south-east of Fishguard off B4329.*

A castle site only, with too few traceable remains to suggest its form, and no known history.

**Castell Machen,** *Machen Upper, Monmouthshire. 4½ miles east-north-east of Caerphilly off A468.*

Castell Machen was an early 13th Century Welsh castle whose buildings and round tower were built on a rocky ridge. A walled bailey stood in front, but the castle is now heavily ruined. It is only mentioned once in documents, as being captured from the Welsh in 1236.

**Castellmarch,** *Abersoch, Caernarvonshire. 5 miles south-west of Pwllheli off A499.*

Castellmarch was originally a fine 17th Century mansion, and though its remains now simply form a farmhouse, parts of its character remain—such as the thick oak rafters. According to legend, this was the site of the castle of King March who had been cursed with horse's ears. The only people who knew this were his barbers, so to preserve the secret of his shame, King March had every barber that cut his hair put to death immediately afterwards. All the barbers' bodies were buried in the same area where it so happened that excellent and abundant reeds grew. A local piper decided to use these reeds for his pipes, but whenever he blew his new pipes, they sang out the secret of the king. (It should be mentioned that a similar legend is told of an ancient Greek king.)

**Castell Mawr,** *Blaen-waun, Carmarthenshire. 11 miles west-north-west of Carmarthen.*

Some sources list this as the former site of a castle, but recent investigations suggest the traces are probably from prehistoric times.

**Castell Meurig,** *Llangadog, Carmarthenshire. 6 miles north-east of Llandeilo off A4069.*

The site is known, but there are no remains, of the Welsh castle also known as Llangadog Castle (or sometimes spelt Llangadoch, but not to be confused with Llangattock in Monmouthshire). Llangadog was once an important town and its castle was an essential guardian of the lands to the south

and the vital roads—both to the Welsh and the Romans before them. The Normans, however, never bothered to establish a stronghold there, and Castell Meurig's military involvements were largely Welsh feuds. It changed hands in 1203, and again five years later. In 1209 it was destroyed, repaired, then wrecked forever in 1277 when Edward I captured the town.

**Castell Mor Craig,** *Thornhill, Glamorganshire. 5 miles north of Cardiff on A469.*

Enough of Castell Mor Craig's structure remains to trace the arrangements of this Welsh castle on its ridge site—probably because it was apparently never finished and never inhabited, and so never attacked or slighted. The four irregular round towers and the square keep are the work of the mid-13th Century, and it is likely that the castle was begun by Gruffydd ap Rhys of Senghenydd before he was deprived of his lordship in 1267.

**Castell Nantperchellan,** *Cardigan, Cardiganshire. 2 miles south of Cardigan.*

Another misnamed site which is almost certainly not a castle, but an ancient camp.

**Castell Nanhyfer,** *Nevern, Pembrokeshire. 7 miles south-west of Cardigan on B4548.*

Only a little of Castell Nanhyfer (also sometimes referred to as Nevern Castle) now remains, but it was a strong Norman motte and bailey castle. The keep was a small stone square tower and the inner ward was protected by a fine rock ditch. The castle was probably begun in 1191, was captured almost immediately, and recaptured in 1194. After its almost complete destruction in 1195 Nanhyfer was abandoned and a new castle begun at Newport, a short distance to the west. The Pipe Roll of 1197 records money borrowed for repairs  t Castell

Nanhyfer, but this money was probably spent on Newport Castle.

**Castell Nant-yr-Arian,** *Goginan, Cardiganshire. 7 miles east of Aberystwyth off A44.*

The site only of a castle mentioned once in documents as "Old Goginan Castle" but, apparently, never documented again.

**Castell Nantcribba,** *Forden, Montgomeryshire. 4 miles south-south-east of Welshpool between A490 and B4388.*

On a large, conical, rocky hill are the featureless remains of a small stone castle which probably once had four towers. The foot of the rocky rise is surrounded by a large enclosure which is of no great strength, being only moated. The site is one hundred yards east of Offa's Dyke, and appears to have no other history than an association with a castle of Gwyddgrug which was captured in 1264.

**Castell Pen-yr-allt,** *Llantood, Pembrokeshire. 3 miles south-south-east of Cardigan off A487.*

Only earthworks remain to show that Castell Pen-yr-allt was once a large ditched and banked enclosure. It apparently had no motte, but stonework remains may be from the castle tower. There is no known history of the castle.

**Castell Poeth,** *Tref Asser, Pembrokeshire. 4 miles west of Fishguard.*

Another castle site which has no documented history.

**Castell Prysor,** *Trawsfynydd, Merioneth. 4½ miles south-east of Ffestiniog off B4212.*

The site now known as Castell Prysor was mentioned in documents in 1284, though not as a castle, and there appears to be no other mention. Experts have found it impossible to date the motte which has its faces revetted in dry walling, so it is yet another "mystery".

**Castell Tal-y-van,** *Ystradowen, Glamorgan. 2 miles north-north-east of Cowbridge off B4222.*

The greatly ruined oval ward with the wreck of its fallen curtain wall, at Nat. Grid Ref. ST 021772, is all that remains of Castell Tal-y-van. It was probably the successor to the Ystradowen earthwork fortification half a mile away at ST 011776. Documents first mention the castle in 1248, and record it being seized by the Welsh in 1245. It was again mentioned in 1314 and 1315, but may have been destroyed soon after that, as it was not mentioned among the castles which Hugh le Despenser was granted by Edward II, after the king had subdued the barons who had risen against his hated favourite.

**Castell Tan-y-castell,** *Llanfarian, Cardiganshire. 1¼ miles south of Aberystwyth off A487.*

This is the site of the predecessor of Aberystwyth Castle at Nat. Grid Ref. SN 579815. (See Aberystwyth Castle for details of its known history.)

**Castell Tinboeth,** *Llanbister, Radnorshire. 9 miles north-north-east of Llandrindod Wells on A483.*

Except for the fragmented ruin of the old square gate tower, Castell Tinboeth has vanished down to its foundations. Originally, a strong ditch guarded the polygonal enclosure, and it was probably built in the late 13th Century. The castle is recorded in different sources by no less than a dozen names, yet only two mentions in historical documents hint at its history—it was a fully functional castle in 1316, and it was captured in 1322. Nothing has been heard of it since.

**Castell-y-Waun**—*see Chirk Castle.*

**Castle upon Alun,** *St. Bride's Major, Glamorgan. 4 miles south-west of Bridgend.*

These few remains are all that is left of the small fortification that also served as an outpost of Ogmore Castle.

**Castle Caereinion,** *Castle Caereinion, Montgomeryshire. 4 miles west-south-west of Welshpool on B4385.*

Castle Caereinion had a brief history, and now nothing more than the site of its motte may be seen. It was built in 1156, but captured and destroyed only eleven years later. That, apparently, was the end of fortifications on this site.

**Castle Ditches,** *Llantwit Major, Glamorgan. On coast 9½ miles west of Barry.*

It does not seem as if there was ever a castle here, but certainly it was a fortified site at some distant date—probably the Iron Age. The traces of a camp on the hill, and the ditches of earthworks indicate that the river mouth was at one time fortified. Some of this work may have been carried out by the Romans, for a large example of a Roman villa settlement was found in 1888 near Llantwit, at Caermaed.

**Castle Nimble,** *Old Radnor, Radnorshire. 12 miles east of Llandrindod Wells.*

There are many references to a motte and bailey castle at Old Radnor, but there are faint traces of the earthworks of two castles, at Nat. Grid Refs. SO 248594 and SO 250590. The documents could refer to Castle Nimble, or Old Radnor Castle. Perhaps one was a site never fully occupied—at any rate it was probably built in the early 12th Century. It was first mentioned in 1196, and was largely destroyed later that same year, only to be repaired again. It had a turbulent history: captured in 1215; destroyed again in 1216, and yet again in 1231. Expenditure records mention extensive repairs in 1233, but later entries almost certainly refer to New Radnor Castle at SO 212610, nearly three miles away.

**Castle Tump,** *Trecastle, Carmarthenshire. 10 miles west of Brecon on A40.*

These are scanty remains of what was probably a motte and bailey castle. The castle would have had an important role—the town was once of considerable stature, an important stop on the road from Brecon to Fishguard and Milford Haven.

**Cas Troggy,** *Llantrisant, Monmouthshire. 8¼ miles north-east of Newport.*

The greatly ruined remains of what was a small castle, built initially as a tower in 1305. It is possible that the castle was never finished and that it was used more as a hunting lodge than a structure of defence. There was a hall between the two towers, both large but one very large and probably polygonal. The rest of the castle was, it seems, built with very inferior masonry, and is totally ruined.

**Cefyn-y-Castell,** *Middletown, Montgomeryshire. 6 miles north-east of Welshpool off A458.*

Perhaps a Roman camp or an ancient hill fort

once stood here, but no known castle. Cefyn-y-Castell is really the correct name for the hill in The Breiddens which is often known as Middle-Town Hill. It overlooks Shropshire, and perhaps in the first half of the first century Caractacus paused here in his retreat from the Roman advance across the eastern lands.

Cefyn-y-Castell rises above the home of Old Parr, who was born in Edward IV's reign and died, reputedly aged 153, in the reign of Charles I. Perhaps he would have lived even longer, but Charles I was intrigued by his longevity, and Old Parr was taken to London to meet the king. The excitement, the long journey (and perhaps London's air) proved too much for the old man—he died soon after and was buried in Westminster Abbey.

**Cefnllys Castle,** *Llandrindod Wells, Radnorshire. 2 miles east of Llandrindod Wells.*

The precipitous hill east of this mid-Wales town has been the site of more than one fortification. The top of the lofty ridge is encircled by a strong rampart forming a large elongated enclosure which was probably a hill fort. At the north end of the enclosure are traces of a stone castle which seems to have had a keep of some sort. A strong ditch divides the enclosure, and at the southern end are the remains of a compact small castle, which had a round tower.

The site of the fortifications is believed to have belonged to the princes of South Wales, and a silver thumb-ring dug up there may have been the signet ring of one of the princes, but the history of the whole site is much confused. Ralph Mortimer, Earl of Wigmore and Lord of Maelienydd, may have begun a castle here in 1242. Documents first mention Cefnllys in 1246, and there was considerable destruction in 1262. In 1273–74 the castle was completely rebuilt—almost as a new castle, apparently, and this may have been when it was moved to the southern end. Cefnllys Castle was captured in 1322, and listed as defensible in Henry IV's surveys of the defences of Wales in 1403.

**Chepstow Castle,** *Chepstow, Monmouthshire. North end of town near river off A48.*

If there have been few dramatic or highly colourful events in Chepstow Castle's history, that history is nevertheless interesting for its length and its association with a vast number of characters and happenings. It has had a number of major periods of building and rebuilding, was in constant use for six hundred years from the Norman Conquest until after the Reformation, and was still partly occupied when Nelson died off Cape Trafalgar.

Chepstow Castle was founded by William Fitz-Osbern, the Norman Lord of Breteuil who was made Earl of Hereford by William the Conqueror. In the few years between the invasion and his death in 1071, FitzOsbern aggressively pushed his Hereford boundary westwards, and since the castle lies immediately inside the Welsh border on the River Wye where the main route to South Wales crossed, it was probably begun in 1067 to act as a base from which deeper penetrations into Wales could be made. The site also commanded a harbour, so it was ideally placed for provisioning the Earl's expeditions, and its strategic importance is reflected in its being one of the earliest masonry Norman castles in Britain (though the rocky site made this construction far more feasible than at many other sites). By the time the Earl died he had subdued most of what is now Monmouthshire, and the castle no doubt played a leading part in these campaigns.

The earldom of Hereford—and with it Chepstow Castle—was taken from William's son Roger of Breteuil in 1075 after his actions in an attempted rebellion against William I (Roger was also sentenced to "perpetual" imprisonment), and stayed in royal hands until 1115. The castle then went to Walter FitzRichard, of the Clare family, as part of a massive area of land (covering what is now Monmouthshire and Gloucestershire) granted by Henry I to create the lordship marcher of Striguil, which survived until Henry VIII incorporated the marcher estates into the realm. (Striguil was the old Welsh name for Chepstow, and is derived from a word meaning "the bend"—the River Wye makes a sharp bend as it passes the town).

Even sixty years after it was begun Chepstow was still an adequate stronghold, and Walter seems to have made no additions. Not that he was inactive in his lordship—he is now mainly remembered as the founder of Tintern Abbey, begun in 1131. Walter died without an heir in 1138, and King Stephen granted the lordship to Walter's nephew Gilbert, the first "Strongbow". He died in 1148, being succeeded by Richard de Clare, the second "Strongbow", and conqueror of Leinster. Henry II, annoyed by Richard's Irish adventures, took over Chepstow Castle and his other Welsh castles in 1170; but soon returned them, for Chepstow was again in Strongbow's hands when the area was raided by Hywel ap Iorwerth in 1173. Henry once again held Striguil castles and lands in 1176—this time, however, as ward for Isabella, Richard's unmarried daughter and heir. She lived in Chepstow Castle protected by a royal constable, a chaplain and his clerk, a porter, three watchmen, ten men-

at-arms, ten archers, and a further fifteen men-at-arms for whom the castle was their base camp.

Isabella married William Marshall, famous as an outstanding soldier, in 1189, and the defences of Chepstow (and of Pembroke, another of Isabella's castles) were soon brought up to date. Unfortunately little is known about other events at the castle during Earl William's time, and perhaps little but building went on—though Henry III stayed there for a few days in the summer of 1217. Two years later the Earl died and was succeeded in turn by his five sons, all of whom were to die childless. They did, however, inherit their father's enthusiasm for building and made a large number of additions to the castle's accommodation and defence. Only the son Richard's lordship saw work on the castle disrupted—by a dispute with Henry, who kept the castle in his own hands for a while in 1231. The dispute was settled when the king paid a second visit to Chepstow Castle in December the following year; but once again it flared up, and Richard went to Ireland, where he was murdered, in April 1234. The next brother, Gilbert, also met a violent end, being killed in a tournament in 1241. Then came Walter, and finally Anselm who inherited the castle, and died, in the same year—1245.

Earl William had five daughters as well as five sons, and on Anselm's death the lordship of Striguil was partitioned and the lands divided among the sisters —Maud, the eldest, getting Chepstow Castle with the southern lands. She eventually had a son, Roger Bigod II, who became Earl of Norfolk, but he was too busy with East Anglian affairs to bother much about Chepstow. Roger Bigod III, however, was much more interested in Wales, and being a lord marcher gave him a chance to play a prominent part in the reign of Edward I. He made many vital additions and improvements to Chepstow Castle, put up the town walls, and rebuilt the church at Tintern Abbey. With only one break of five or six years (while the town walls were being put up) work on the castle went on for thirty years after 1270, though much was already completed by the end of 1285 in time for a visit from Edward I— whose Welsh wars Chepstow survived unmarked, being far too remote from the conflict.

Another turning point in the castle's life came when Roger's brother John inherited it. He was

*Opposite: Chepstow, 12th Century hold of the powerful barons Gilbert and Richard de Clare—both surnamed "Strongbow" for their prowess in war*

greatly in debt and the temptation of an annuity for life was strong enough for him to agree that at the end of it his lands would pass to the crown. He died in 1306, and Edward I wasted no time in taking possession, putting the castle in the care of appointed royal constables. One of these, from 1308–10, after Edward II came to the throne, was Hugh le Despenser, who carried out many repairs. As with so many other places, for Chepstow Castle there are few pleasant or honourable memories of Edward II's reign. The castle came to belong to two of the king's brothers, but the deputy constable in charge looted the castle, and even in the direct care of one of the brothers, Thomas de Brotherton, it deteriorated badly. Hugh le Despenser bought the castle again in 1323—another addition to his vast South Wales territory. But the years of power were rapidly drawing to a close for Despenser and his king, and at the end of 1326 Chepstow surrendered without a siege, and the hated Despenser was executed. After that it went back to Thomas de Brotherton, and eventually in 1399 to Thomas Mowbray, Duke of Norfolk, after three quarters of a century of quiet obscurity.

Owain Glyndwr's rising brought the castle's military purpose back to the fore, and in 1403 it was garrisoned with 20 men-at-arms and 60 archers— a formidable force, since a castle as important as Harlech had only half as many. The size of the garrison obviously put off the rebels, for though most of the present county suffered greatly, Chepstow was unmolested. In 1405 Thomas Mowbray was executed for treason, and eventually, in 1468, the castle landed in the hands of William Herbert, Lord of Raglan and Earl of Pembroke. His granddaughter married the bastard son of Henry, Duke of Somerset and Earl of Worcester, whose family owned the castle until the present century.

For a period of over 300 years almost the only building carried out was on domestic sections; and by 1627 Chepstow Castle had become practically a great house, with very inadequate and antiquated defences, under Henry, 5th Earl and 1st Marquis of Worcester. This was unfortunate, because the castle was about to enter the most strenuous stage of its military life. The Marquis was an ardent Royalist and on the outbreak of the Civil War held the castle for Charles I; but in April 1643, fearing the advancing Parliamentarians, the town and the castle were abandoned. This turned out to be a very premature move, and the castle was reoccupied and held again for the king. The Parliamentarians duly made preparations to attack and besiege Chepstow with a force of 1,300 from their Monmouth garrison, but a Royalist attack on Monmouth sent them back. By October, 1645, however, the Royalists were practically beaten. Monmouth fell, and the Chepstow garrison surrendered after only a token resistance.

The castle withstood a second siege with more determination during the second Civil War, when Sir Nicholas Kemeys and 120 men held out against the personal direction of Cromwell, who eventually carried on westward, leaving the castle besieged. The defence was good, but Cromwell's guns breached the wall, and with it the garrison's morale. Far less determined to hold out than Sir Nicholas, members of the garrison rushed out through the breach and surrendered individually. After a final assault the castle fell and Sir Nicholas was killed, either in the battle, or in cold blood after it. (There is another account which suggests that the castle only gave in when all supplies were exhausted, and after a Parliamentarian soldier had swum the Wye and cut loose the boat which was the last hope of escape for the Royalist garrison.) Chepstow Castle was not slighted after the Civil Wars, but was granted to Cromwell who repaired it and kept it garrisoned until the Restoration in 1660, when Charles II appointed as custodian Lord Herbert, son of the rightful owner. A garrison was kept in the castle, and it was still used as a prison. Probably its best known prisoner was the regicide Henry Marten who spent twenty years in Chepstow Castle before he died in 1680. But he could have had little to complain about—his rooms in the large east tower were comfortable (the tower thereafter was known as Marten's Tower), and he was able to tour the countryside with his wife and visit friends.

Orders were given in 1690 for the castle to be dismantled and its guns taken to Chester, but the small garrison had itself already left by the time the order reached Chepstow, and though some destruction did take place, it was far from the intended demolition. Simple deterioration and neglect probably caused as much damage, though at the beginning of the 19th Century Marten's Tower still had its roof, and part of the castle was inhabited. Successors of Henry, Marquis of Worcester (and, since 1682, Duke of Beaufort) held Chepstow Castle until it was sold in 1914 to Mr. W. R. Lysaght. The Ministry of Public Buildings and Works (now the Department of the Environment) was invested with permanent guardianship in 1953.

Chepstow Castle is a substantial ruin and occupies a long narrow ridge running roughly west to east on the southern bank of the River Wye; it is separated from the town by a deep gulley known as the Dingle. At the enclosure's narrowest point, almost at the middle of the castle complex, is the Great Tower, the lower part of which is the main surviving part of FitzOsbern's 11th Century castle. To the west is the upper bailey with a barbican and upper gatehouse. East of the Great Tower is the middle bailey, and the lower bailey with the great hall, lesser hall, Marten's Tower, the Great Gatehouse, and the site of a barbican.

The middle bailey was added by William Marshall from 1189–1219, and building went on from about a year later until 1245, with the heightening of the Great Tower, rebuilding of the original upper bailey, addition of lower bailey to the east, and finally the western barbican. The domestic buildings in the lower bailey were added in the ten years after 1275, and Marten's Tower took the next eight years. The curtain walls were considerably thickened in 1650 (to carry cannons and withstand enemy artillery), the vast quantities of stone needed leading to the dismantling of many of the interior buildings and most of the upper storey of the Great Tower.

**Chirk Castle,** *Chirk, Denbighshire. 4 miles south-west of Llangollen off B4500.*

Chirk Castle is often known by its Welsh name of Castell-y-Waun (Meadow Castle), and the site was in Welsh hands until Edward I's conquest of 1282. The earliest fortification was known as Castell Crogen, and was built in the 11th Century. The Edwardian castle was probably started in 1283, and was built by one of the Mortimer marcher lords, Roger, who was appointed as a reward for the part he played in the defeat of Llywelyn, the last native Prince of Wales.

Chirk's position on the Welsh border determined that the castle should be a strong one, but although Roger's castle was adequate, its final form was considerably more massive and formidable. Most of the reconstruction and extension was carried out from about 1310, and it resulted in a strong castle with a roughly rectangular plan. The north front was 250 feet long, and at each angle stood a massive round tower, half-round towers being placed on the faces. The battlements were built wide enough to allow two men to walk side by side. The great quadrangle, 160 by 100 feet, is entered through a magnificent archway between two drum towers.

In 1644 Chirk Castle had the unusual distinction of being besieged by its owner. Sir Thomas Myddelton (Lord Mayor of London in 1613) had bought the castle in 1595, and in 1644 his son Thomas, a

*Chirk Castle, its appearance much softened since the days when it was held by the powerful Marcher Lord, Roger Mortimer*

Parliamentarian, found his castle occupied by Royalists. Try as he might, Thomas could not dislodge the Royalists, who remained there until the first Parliamentarian victories of 1646. But then Thomas switched allegiance to Charles I, and in 1659 it was his turn to experience a siege by the Parliamentarian forces. Thomas was no more successful with his defence than he was with his siege, and the Parliamentarian artillery commanded by General Lambert soon made many breaches in Chirk's castle walls. Eventually, when he heard that Parliament had ordered the complete destruction of Chirk Castle, Thomas Myddelton surrendered, and the castle's military life came to an end.

There are many relics of the castle's history—particularly of its unusual Civil War stage—in the storerooms that lead off the quadrangle. A con-

siderable amount of the structure remains, though one complete curtain and its towers have disappeared, either by landslide or by disintegration following extensive damage by Cromwell's guns. There is also much of interest architecturally; one huge room's single-piece beams are so long that the floor "gives" with a noticeable rhythm as you walk across it. There are also numerous paintings of local scenes, and portraits of royalty and other historical figures. The elaborate iron gates guarding the castle grounds were erected between 1719 and 1721, and are notable examples of the craft of the Davies brothers, whose workshop was not far away near Bersham.

**Cilgerran Castle,** *Cilgerran, Pembrokeshire. 2 miles south-south-east of Cardigan.*

On a strong site formed by a precipitous crag above the left bank of the Teifi stand the ruined 13th Century drum towers of Cilgerran Castle—though the history that distinguishes the site precedes the building of the towers by fifty years.

When the Normans invaded South Wales they at first made little headway against Rhys ap Tewdwr, ruler of the Kingdom of Deheubarth (most of South Wales excluding present day Monmouthshire and Glamorgan), and it was only after Rhys's death in 1093 that the Normans were able to settle western Wales and build their castles at Cardigan, Pembroke and Carmarthen. Under Henry I this settlement continued, and one of the marcher lordships established was that of Cilgerran. It was held by Gerald de Windsor, who was also granted Pembroke Castle. Gerald's wife, the beautiful Nest (daughter of Rhys, Prince of South Wales) who inspired so many tales and legends, was abducted from a castle known as Cenarth Bychan by Cadwgan of Powys. This started a bitter feud between the Norman and Cadwgan, and Henry gave Gerald special favours and territories to carry out

his vengeance. The site of Cenarth Bychan quite likely became the site of Cilgerran Castle, though there are five 12th Century motte and bailey sites in the area.

Deheubarth became established once again in the chaotic years after Henry's death, so that nineteen years later Henry II found it impossible to restore Norman influence in West Wales. Then, in 1164, the Lord Rhys, grandson of Rhys ap Tewdwr, captured Cardigan; Cilgerran fell to him a year later, and he won numerous concessions from the King. Rhys died in 1197 and a long and bitter dispute among his sons over the succession caused the final break-up of the Kingdom of Deheubarth— the final blow coming in 1204 when William Marshall, Earl of Pembroke (see Chepstow Castle), captured Cilgerran. Not that he held it for long, however, for Llywelyn the Great confirmed his overlordship of the numerous Welsh princes by capturing the whole of Pembroke. After this victory at Cilgerran, Llywelyn was able to reconcile Rhys's sons, and so unify South and North Wales in the Council of All Wales at Aberystwyth.

Llywelyn's hold over Cilgerran Castle was also shortlived, for in 1223 William Marshall's eldest son, another William, recaptured the castle. He began to rebuild it with the same enthusiasm that all his family seemed to have for building (Chepstow also underwent extensive reconstruction at this time), and the surviving remains date from this era. This was also the last time the castle was to have a forced change of hands for nearly 200 years, though in 1257 Llywelyn, Prince of Wales (grandson of Llywelyn the Great) ravaged the area, and a year later a battle fought near Cilgerran resulted in a Welsh victory.

The remaining medieval years saw much breaking up of the country into new and smaller tenures, and many parts became Crown lordships; though Cilgerran, passing through the hands of each of the younger William Marshall's four brothers, remained independent. Their sister Eva inherited on

*Opposite: The massive towers of Cilgerran Castle. This may have been the site of Cenarth Bychan, the earlier stronghold from which the Welsh chief Cadwgan abducted the beautiful Nest, wife of the Norman lord Gerald de Windsor*

the death in 1245 of Anselm, the last of the great soldier's sons. She was by then the widow of William de Braose, Lord of Abergavenny, and her daughter married William de Cantelupe—so Cilgerran became associated with Abergavenny instead of with Pembroke. Cilgerran Castle was held by the Cantelupes and the related Hastings family right through to the end of the 14th Century, becoming connected with Pembroke again in 1339 when Lawrence de Hastings was granted the earldom by Edward III.

Unfortunately the Cantelupes and Hastings did not look after Cilgerran Castle as carefully as had the Marshalls; by 1275 it had been looted of much of its furnishings, and 50 years later it was reported to be in ruins. Then, in 1372, John de Hastings, Earl of Pembroke, took the fleet to reinforce an English army in Aquitaine, but was defeated at sea by the Spanish fleet. Fearing an invasion, Edward III—in one of his last acts as king—ordered that Cilgerran, Pembroke and Tenby castles should be repaired and strengthened. The lordship of Cilgerran and the earldom of Pembroke were at this time held by the king, since the last of the Hastings family was still a minor. He died a minor too, and the holdings remained with the crown.

War returned to Cilgerran in 1405 during Owain Glyndwr's revolt, and once again the Welsh held Cilgerran Castle's rocky hill—briefly, but still long enough to cause enormous damage, according to subsequent reports. The turbulent and confused years of the 15th Century, particularly during the Wars of the Roses, led to a number of changes in the lordship of Cilgerran and the earldom of Pembroke, but they ended up (for the second time) in the hands of Jasper Tudor after his nephew Henry VII won his victory on Bosworth Field. When Henry VIII abolished the Marcher Lordships in the 1536 Act of Union, Cilgerran was included in Pembrokeshire, and the Vaughans, who had been granted the castle by Henry VII, occupied it until the early 17th Century.

During the Civil War which started in 1642 action in West Wales mainly took place in and around Pembroke, which was one of the comparatively few castles in Wales garrisoned for the Parliamentarians. Although the area saw many battles between the Royalists and Cromwell's soldiers there is no record of Cilgerran Castle being in-

volved, and perhaps it was already too much of a ruin to bother about. When peace returned the castle continued to deteriorate, and eventually it became a romantic ruin favoured by many artists, including Turner and Peter de Wint. In 1930 Cilgerran Castle was acquired by the National Trust, and the Ministry of Public Buildings and Works (now the Department of the Environment) took charge in 1943.

The layout of the castle, surrounded on three sides by steep slopes, seems to follow the earliest motte and bailey plan, an inner ward occupying the traditional site of the motte and defended by a ditch beyond the two massive towers and gatehouse; and an outer ward, guarded by a strong ditch, following the traditional bailey pattern. Cilgerran's appeal is in its setting high above the confluence of the Teifi with the Plysgog stream, and in the attractive balance of the two ruined towers. These, with the few other remains, are sufficient to trace the whole structure, and, above all, to let imagination wander.

**Clyro Castle,** *Clyro, Radnorshire. 1 mile northwest of Hay-on Wye, at junction of A4153 and B4351.*

A part of a moat, a small mound, and numerous indications of masonry reveal the rather shapeless plan of a vanished castle that in Henry IV's review of 1403 was still a defensible stronghold. It was probably a Norman castle, and used a natural hillock for much of its defensive position. In the reign of Elizabeth I a fortified mansion was built here, but that too was destroyed—by fire. Its original gateway survived, and is now a farm entrance.

**Coity Castle,** *Coity, Glamorgan. 1½ miles north-east of Bridgend.*

The legend of Coity Castle's early days might be based on uncertain evidence, but legends survive for reasons other than accuracy. In the Norman conquest of Glamorgan one of the knights accompanying Robert FitzHamon was Payn de Turbeville. After FitzHamon (founder of Cardiff Castle) had given lands to eleven other knights for their services, so the legend runs, Payn asked where his lands were to be. But instead he was given men and arms, and told to get them where he could. So he came to Coity, where he asked the Welsh chieftain Morgan to surrender his castle. Morgan's reply was to bring out his daughter Sybil, and to tell Payn that if he would marry Sybil, he could enter and keep the castle. If he would not have her, the castle's fate would be settled by a duel between Morgan and Payn. Payn handed his sword to Morgan with his left hand, holding it by the blade; with his right arm he embraced Sybil. Soon they were married and Payn moved into Coity Castle, switching his allegiance to Caradoc ap Jestyn and

*Coity Castle; there is a romantic legend associated with the first Norman knight reputed to have held the castle*

maintaining a formidable force of Welshmen with Morgan's aid.

So much for the legend: but it is true that Payn de Turbeville was in Glamorgan in 1126, and that his descendants held Coity many years later. If the legend is untrue, it may partly owe its conception to the start of the earliest masonry castle on the site. Its builder was Sir Gilbert de Turbeville (who held the fief at the beginning of the 13th Century) and he married Maud, daughter of the Welsh Lord of Avan, Morgan Gam.

The male Turbevilles came to an end in the 14th Century and the territories were divided up, and Coity many years later came into the ownership of Sir William Gamage. He had the misfortune to be in his castle when Owain Glyndwr attacked Glamorgan, with a siege of Coity as part of his plans for revolt in 1403. So prolonged was the siege that it aroused the concern of the Commons who requested Henry IV to see to the rescue of the Lord of Coity. Nearly 200 years later, at the end of the 16th Century, the male line of the Gamages also died out, and Sir Robert Sidney, later the 2nd Earl of Leicester, gained Coity Castle when he married Barbara Gamage in 1584—though this property must have been of little consequence to him, as the deserted castle began to decay from this period.

Today Coity Castle is the picturesque ruin of a large outer ward and a round inner ward. The almost square keep, 40 by 35 feet, and most of the curtain wall of the inner ward are the oldest parts, and date from the 12th Century. A tower was built out of the southern curve of this wall in the 13th Century, to give a better flanking defence, the substantial keep in the north-west arc of the curtain guarding the gentler slope of that side. There was a great deal of building in the 14th Century, which almost amounted to rebuilding the castle. Newly constructed in this phase were: the east gate house in the inner ward curtain, a heightening of parts of this wall, the wall enclosing the irregular outer ward, a middle gate just south of the keep linking the two wards, the improved interior of the keep, a chapel, and various domestic buildings in the inner ward. In Tudor times the moat which originally encircled the whole inner ward was filled in where it ran through the outer ward, and a four-floor annexe was added to the north-west side of the keep.

**Colwyn Castle,** *Hundred House, Radnorshire. 5 miles east-north-east of Builth Wells on A481.*

Scant remains, with nothing standing above ground, of a ringwork castle with a strong counterscarp bank inside a rectangular enclosure. It may have been an early 12th Century Welsh castle which has been listed, probably after its capture by the English, as being restored in 1144, "destroyed" in 1196, and captured again in 1215.

**Conway Castle,** *Conway, Caernarvonshire. South-east edge of town off A55.*

If any castle rivals Caernarvon's fame as a masterpiece of military engineering and superb design, it is Conway Castle. And if one includes in any comparison the walls of the town itself, then Conway is unsurpassed throughout Europe. Like Caernarvon (and Harlech) it was begun in 1283, after Edward I's second campaign in Wales had ended with the death of Llywelyn, Prince of Wales, the capture of his brother Dafydd, and the end of Welsh hopes of independence. Like Caernarvon it still stands, nearly 700 years later, as a staggering monument to the relentless determination of Edward, and to the skill of the castle's planners and builders. Foremost among these was the Master of the King's Works in Wales, James of St. George, whose skill Edward called upon for most of his Welsh castles, as well as for many buildings in England.

The work of this designer and mason from Savoy would be impressive enough if only the military aspects were examined. Yet despite the large number of buildings with which he was involved, James still managed to combine functionality with varied and impressive appearance. To a considerable extent the sites influenced design—there is simply no room for a concentric castle at Conway or Caernarvon, and so the plan of Conway resembles Caernarvon far more than it resembles Harlech. But whereas Caernarvon Castle took some 40 years to build, and even then was not finished, Conway was garrisoned by 1285 (in which year there were 1,500 craftsmen and labourers at work), almost completed five years later, and expenditure seems to have stopped four years after that. Probably none too soon either, for Conway turned out to be the most expensive building programme begun by the king, costing in today's terms at least £2½ million.

Conway Castle was built on a broad, steep-sided rock at the south-east edge of the town, bordered on one side by the river Conway and on another by Gyffin brook. In the roughly triangular plan of the old town defences, the length of the almost oblong castle blunts the apex of the triangle. The castle walls are in places fifteen feet thick, and link eight massive round towers, in noticeable contrast to Caernarvon Castle's many angles. Each tower was originally surmounted by a prominent round turret, but only four of these remain, on the four towers marking the square inner ward which forms the eastern section of the castle.

There were two entrances to Conway Castle. Only a few steps remain of the closed-up gateway in the eastern barbican—formerly a long and narrow flight cut into the rock and leading down the steep bank to the river. The main entrance was by a ramp leading to a drawbridge and so into the narrow western barbican. The gateway between the two western towers led into the outer ward, which contained the great hall and accommodation and kitchens for the garrison and lesser officers. A defended middle gate led to the inner ward and its more elaborate domestic rooms, including the state rooms built for Edward and Queen Eleanor —the King's Chamber, the King's Hall, and a chapel among them.

Holding Conway was an important part of Edward's plan to form a defensive ring around Snowdon, and seal off Anglesey—both haunts of Welsh leaders—and this must have speeded its construction. The route to the sea through the Vale of Conway had been won when the Welsh castle at Dolwyddelan was captured, and in spring 1283, when work on Conway Castle was in its early stages, Edward and Queen Eleanor camped at Aberconway. Local legend claimed that they were there when the head of Llywelyn was brought to them, but this almost certainly happened at Rhuddlan Castle (see also Aberedw Castle).

Another local legend was sufficiently believed for a plaque based upon it to be set in the chapel when it was rededicated to Queen Victoria. The plaque portrays Queen Eleanor and recalls that she and the king spent Christmas 1290 at the castle—unfortunately, Eleanor had by then been dead and buried over a month, and Edward was in seclusion near London. But Edward was certainly there in 1294, though he doubtless wished he was somewhere else. He had come personally to direct the subduing of Prince Madoc's sudden uprising, and arrived at Conway Castle with a small retinue, well ahead of his main force. Then the Welsh rebels noticed that a swollen river had delayed the English soldiers, and they rapidly surrounded and besieged the castle. The siege seems to have gone on for a few days—there is an account of Edward being compelled to eat such unroyal food as salted meat and coarse bread, and to wash it down with water sweetened with honey—and the capture of the castle cannot have been far off. But just in time the river subsided, and the main force was able to drive off the besiegers.

The highest compliment one can pay a defensive stronghold is never even to attempt to attack it— which indicates why the largest and most impressive castles seldom have the colourful and eventful military history which often attaches to smaller holds. With Llywelyn and Dafydd dead, and with the minor risings which followed doomed to failure, the massive castles must have been grim and ever-present reminders to the Welsh of a power they could not hope to match. A peace of sorts, however unwanted, was inevitable. So it was that, like Caernarvon, Conway Castle began to seem redundant and soon showed signs of neglect. What maintenance was carried out was haphazard, and when Edward III's son, the Black Prince, became Prince of Wales and inherited his Welsh lands, a survey of Conway Castle revealed that many of the roofs were unsafe. This resulted in practically the only major work of the mid-14th Century—replacing wooden roof trusses with stone arches.

The sad tale of the end of Richard II's reign closely concerns Conway Castle. When Richard (the Black Prince's son) returned from Ireland—where he had gone after the murder of the recognised heir to the throne—he made for Conway: it was then regarded as impregnable, and here the bewildered monarch hoped to find security. His Welsh followers had deserted, however, and the castle was unprovisioned. By now almost alone, Richard welcomed into Conway Henry Percy, Earl of Northumberland, who had come to the king as emissary from the cousin Richard so feared, Henry Bolingbroke, Duke of Lancaster. Under the assurance that Henry only wanted him to go to London to summon Parliament, and with the sworn promise of safe conduct, Richard left Conway with Northumberland to meet Bolingbroke, who was travelling from Chester. But not far from the castle (and not at all to Northumberland's surprise) they were ambushed, and Richard was taken to Flint Castle. There he was persuaded to renounce the throne; Bolingbroke became Henry IV, and within a year Richard was dead. These events were traditionally prophesied by Merlin, the Welsh wizard, who foresaw a king of Albion, after reigning for 20 years, being " undone in the parts of the north in a triangular place "—Richard's reign and Conway's plan and location fitting these descriptions.

Conway was again the scene of trickery only two years later, when on a day in 1401 that happened to be All Fool's Day as well as Good Friday, a man calling himself a carpenter was admitted at the castle gate. Almost the whole garrison of 75 was at church, and the "carpenter" let in a band of fellow Welsh rebels, led by the brothers Gwylyn and Rhys Tewdwr. Seizing the castle, they proclaimed their loyalty to their prince, Owain Glyndwr—thus carrying out one of that rebellion's most audacious exploits. Hopeless as their cause eventually became, they won a pardon for most of their number from " Harry Hotspur ", in exchange for the castle and the imprisonment of nine of them.

Early in the Wars of the Roses an event occurred which the local Welsh took much pleasure in remembering, even though the slain soldier, too, was Welsh. Conway was then held by Yorkists, and facing a probable attack by Lancastrian forces. A Lancastrian officer, studying the castle's defences

from a rise half a mile away across the river, was killed by an arrow shot by one of the castle's defenders, Llywelyn of Nannau. Unfortunately there is no record of Llywelyn repeating this remarkable feat of archery.

For nearly 200 years Conway Castle's history is undistinguished by events of note, and it gradually became more and more dilapidated, so that in 1628 it was sold for only £100 to Viscount Conway. At this time there came into prominence in the town one of the most distinguished men ever born there —John Williams, Archbishop of York. He was much admired by Charles I, and more than returned the admiration, for after the Civil War broke out in 1642 the Archbishop began to repair and fortify Conway Castle at his own expense, garrisoning it for the king. Unfortunately his dedicated and honourable character was not shared by the governor of the castle, Sir John Owen, who took over most of the goods put in the Archbishop's care by trusting local Welshmen. In 1646 the Parliamentarians led by Major-General Mytton (the captor of Caernarvon Castle), besieged Conway. With Charles I already handed over to Parliament by the Scots, and Royalist armies defeated almost everywhere, the town surrendered, and three months later the castle also gave in to Mytton.

On the Restoration in 1660 Charles II restored Conway Castle to the 3rd Earl of Conway, but the years of assault and neglect had taken their toll and left the castle in a very bad state. The Earl began its demolition, and pretending that he was following the king's request, ordered all iron, timber and lead to be removed and shipped to Ireland (where he would be able to sell whatever he did not use on his other estates). But fate outwitted the Earl, for the ship carrying the valuable material sank in a storm on the Irish Sea. Responsibility for the castle was eventually vested in the Local Authority late in the 19th Century, and passed to the Government in 1953. It is cared for by the Department of the Environment, which has carried out much restoration.

Conway Castle still appears a towering, powerful stronghold, and the symmetry of the eight round towers which project so fully from the walls, have captured the imagination of many artists. Conway also presents one of the finest examples of a complete town defensive system that can be found any-where. The town walls are impressive enough on their own—about 1,400 yards in extent, with three double gateways and twenty-one towers. Their average is over 24 feet, and their thickness varies, becoming thinner as they approach the protection of the castle. Like Caernarvon Castle, from the out-side Conway Castle still appears to be almost intact while inside its walls it is ruined. But most of the towers can be climbed, and impressive views can be seen from them and from the walls. Inside the castle one of the most striking features is a solitary stone arch, one of eight that supported the roof of the aptly named Great Hall which was 125 feet long and 30 feet high, and is also notable

*Conway Castle, a fascinating surviving example of medieval castle and town defences combined. The castle was captured by Owain Glyndwr's rebels in 1401*

for its bowed south front which skirts an outcrop of rock.

**Craig-y-Nos Castle,** *Craig-y-Nos, Breconshire. 12 miles north-north-east of Neath on A4067.*

Not a castle, but an indulgence of someone who admired Scottish baronial manors enough to erect a copy in the mountains of Wales. It was bought, and vastly improved, by the Victorian prima donna Adelina Patti, who at the height of her career could readily command £1,000 for a performance. Craig-y-Nos became a peaceful retreat for her and her second (and subsequently, third) husband; she reached it by special train which stopped at Penwyllt, where a luxuriously furnished waiting room was at her disposal. Madame Patti died in 1919 and the "castle" was handed over to the Welsh National Memorial Association to be converted into a hospital. Her elaborate Winter Gardens are now known as the Patti Pavilion, and have been transported to Victoria Park, Swansea.

**Criccieth Castle,** *Criccieth, Caernarvonshire. On sea front near town, 16 miles south of Caernarvon off A497.*

Even in its ruined state it is readily apparent that Criccieth Castle displays two distinct styles, and recent investigations have made clear many of the anomalies of the site. Basically Criccieth Castle is an Edwardian inner ward inside an irregular, early Welsh outer ward set on the crest of an isolated headland between two beaches. In showing so clearly its two different origins Criccieth is something of a rarity, as most Welsh castles which changed hands in the 13th Century either stayed much as they were, or were almost totally obscured by English rebuilding. At Criccieth the outer ward is so ruined that comparatively little is above

ground level; but there is enough left to show its similarity with the less destroyed Welsh castle at Dolwyddelan, on the other side of the mountains of Snowdonia.

The outer ward, with at least two towers, and possibly a third, was probably complete early in the 13th Century, when the ruler in the north was Llywelyn ap Iorwerth (The Great), whose headquarters were at Dolwyddelan Castle. In the castle were once imprisoned Llywelyn's eldest son Gruffydd and his grandson Llywelyn ap Gruffydd, who became Prince of Wales. They were sent there by a council of Welsh princes for refusing to acknowledge the supremacy of the English Crown as Llywelyn the Great had in 1239, a year before his death. So Gruffydd was prevented from succeeding his father, and the last major effort to keep Wales a separate kingdom was left to his son.

The Prince doubtless stayed voluntarily at Criccieth Castle many times after 1239, and in greater comfort, and one of his few surviving letters to Edward I was sent from Criccieth in 1273. One of the towers of the castle came to be called the Mounfort Tower, and could well have been named after the Montfort family, Simon de Montfort once being an ally of Llywelyn's, whose daughter Llywelyn married. Near the end of 1282, during Edward's second Welsh campaign, Llywelyn died at the hands of an insignificant English soldier near Builth. Only a couple of months later Edward captured Dolwydellan Castle, and not long after took Criccieth as well.

Criccieth was well placed for Edward, who wanted to confine the Welsh with a ring of castles round the mountains of the north, and to cut off South and West Wales from the north and Anglesey—and it had the extra advantage of being on the coast. Edward strengthened parts of the outer ward, but the main work was the building of a complete inner ward with a substantial twin-towered gatehouse. The towers appear incongruous on this relatively small site, but they could obviously have served as strongholds themselves, like keeps. The outer ward continued to be protected by two Welsh towers, and by an Edwardian tower on the outer wall, where the new wall continued the line of the Welsh structure. This section of wall and its tower (the Leyburn, or south-east tower) were probably built on top of previous Welsh work. The gatehouse was given additional strength by making it very awkward to approach, being at the opposite end of the site from the gateway in the outer wall. Besides that, it could only be reached by a long walk through the narrow and easily defendable gap between the outer and inner walls on the west side. Experts have noticed a strong similarity between the gatehouse towers and the towers at Harlech Castle which were built by the master-mason William of Drogheda—a similarity made more meaningful by ancient records which show that the busiest building period at Criccieth (1287–88) was the slackest period at nearby Harlech.

Building at Criccieth seems to have continued for many years, and the castle was still being worked on in the reign of Edward II. This was fairly common, as castles fell into disrepair if they were neglected, and improvements were always being made as siege methods grew more sophisticated. But in the summer of 1283 the initial building was urgent enough for the first Edward to send considerable sums of money to Criccieth (from Aberconway, where he had established his headquarters) despite the enormous sums being spent on Conway, Caernarvon and Harlech—almost £5 million in today's terms. The king stayed at Criccieth Castle in August of that year, and again three or four times the following year, when Sir William Leyburn was appointed constable of the castle. Out of his annual fee of £100 (about £14,000 today), Sir William had to pay the garrison of ten crossbowmen, chaplain, armourer, mason, blacksmith, and carpenter, and a number of watchmen, porters, and other serving men.

Criccieth escaped involvement in the 1288 rising of Rhys ap Maredudd (whose father Llywelyn had imprisoned at Criccieth until he swore allegiance); but in Madoc's revolt of 1294—in which Caernarvon fell to the Welsh—the coastal garrisons of mid-Wales were cut off from the land routes to other strongholds. However, the Welsh had no control over sea routes, and Criccieth and Harlech castles were provisioned (although infrequently) by ships. With the Criccieth Castle garrison at that time were nine settlers from the small town, and since there was no town hall. the settlement's thirteen women and nineteen children would have used the castle as a refuge.

Eventually the rising was crushed and Madoc

taken prisoner, and the next break in Criccieth's routine was the confinement in the castle of a batch of prisoners from Edward's invasion of Scotland in 1296. Eleven years later Edward II came to the throne, and during most of his reign there was construction work going on at the castle —heightening towers, general repairs, and so on— and many of the workmen named in the records about this time appeared only a short while previously in Caernarvon Castle's accounts.

Concern about the strength of the castles in Wales (and elsewhere) was revived when Edward III had to contend with new wars with Scotland, and the start of the Hundred Years War in 1338 increased military awareness. When his son Edward (the Black Prince) became Prince of Wales, a survey of all the Welsh castles was carried out, and Criccieth was well provisioned and stocked with adequate arms, these including almost 5,000 iron heads for crossbow bolts. In 1359 the Prince of Wales appointed Criccieth Castle's first Welsh constable, Sir Hywel ap Gruffydd, who had apparently been knighted for gallantry when he fought with Prince Edward at Crécy. His long tenure—until he died about twenty years later—became known (and remembered long after) as Criccieth's brightest and kindest years.

The long years of peace came to an end with Owain Glyndwr's bid for an independent Wales in 1400, and Criccieth Castle was brought into condition and re-garrisoned—Prince Henry (who became Henry V) authorising the castle's establishment in 1402 to be six men-at-arms and fifty archers. Then Harlech Castle, within sight across Tremadoc Bay, was heavily besieged, and both castles were once again cut off from supply by land. But this time they could not rely on the sea. The French were supporting Glyndwr, and the blockade became total when a French fleet sailed into the Irish Sea. A Criccieth defender tried without success to reach Conway for help, and at this Harlech gave up, its provisions gone and its spirit broken. Not long after, Criccieth Castle surrendered as well.

That was the end of its history, too, for Owain Glyndwr did no more than set fire to the castle in the short time that was left before his revolt died. Originally built by the Welsh, and now destroyed by the Welsh, Criccieth Castle crumbled undisturbed for centuries, playing no part at all in the

Civil Wars. Its first repairs were probably those of 1858, carried out by the Ormsby Gore family who bought the castle from the Crown. In 1904 the site was surveyed, and the ruins were cleared and thoroughly examined in the 1930s by the Inspectorate of Ancient Monuments. This examination revealed a number of 13th and 14th Century relics, tools, and weapons. In 1933 Lord Harlech, father of the present Lord Harlech, placed the site under the Government's guardianship, the Department of the Environment now caring for its conservation.

**Crickhowell Castle,** *Crickhowell, Breconshire. In town, 12 miles south-east of Brecon on A40.*

Ivy now covers the ruined towers of Crickhowell Castle which at its height had a shell keep on a motte, a shell gatehouse, and stone wall, with towers, circling the outer ward. It is likely that it was a castle site—as a motte and bailey castle—before the stone keep was erected in the 13th Century, and the gatehouse and two towers of the outer ward were the last additions, probably in the 14th Century. It was briefly taken from the English in 1322, and was still a defensible castle in the review of defences in 1403.

**Cwm Camlais Castle,** *Felin-Camlais, Breconshire. 5¼ miles west-south-west of Brecon.*

Cwm Camlais was a small castle, also known at times as Camlais, Maescar, Blaencamlais, or Defynoch Castle. Very little of its structure now remains, but enough to show that its rocky motte supported a round tower, and that the only outer defence was a counterscarp bank. Apart from a reference that it was destroyed in 1265 (and apparently never repaired), the history of Cwm Camlais is uncertain. Another record is of a "new castle beyond Brecon" built by Llywelyn ap Gruffydd, Prince of Wales, and this quite likely refers to Cwm Camlais Castle.

**Cyfarthfa Castle,** *Merthyr Tydfil, Glamorgan. On the northern edge of the town on A470.*

Cyfarthfa Castle is another modern building which has been built to recall the romantic image of medieval years. It was constructed in 1825 for Robert Thompson Crawshay, the last "Iron King" of Merthyr before the Bessemer process revolutionised the iron industry. Crawshay was a colourful character who entertained lavishly, and many famous people of that Victorian era visited Cyfarthfa Castle. He built a curious church nearby, which has a most unusual tower. Crawshay was also an excellent early photographer, and the museum at the castle has many interesting exhibits.

D

**Deganwy Castle,** *Deganwy, Caernarvonshire. 2 miles south of Llandudno on A496.*

The scanty remains of Deganwy Castle (sometimes called Gannock Castle) occupy two large volcanic outcrops which are close together and form a hill behind the village. The ruins show that the castle builders carefully used the site's unusual character to increase their defensive strength. The larger outcrop carried a small ward guarded by at least three round towers. This outcrop was joined by a double line of defence (it was never completed in stone) to the smaller hillock on which stood a large D-shaped tower. Between the two hillocks, on one line of the linking defence, was the entrance—a large double-towered gatehouse.

Most of the present remains date from the early and middle 13th Century, but Deganwy was a fortified site long before that. The first fortification is said to have been built early in the 6th Century, by the important Welsh ruler Maelgwn, King of Gwynedd. Sometime at the beginning of the 9th Century lightning apparently caused much damage, but it must have been repaired in time for its mention in old documents as a fortification in A.D. 822.

The Norman Hugh de Lupus, Earl of Chester, took over the site in 1088 and rebuilt the fort as a castle. This building was destroyed by Llywelyn the Great when he attacked it in 1241. Another Earl of Chester, under the command of Henry III, rebuilt the castle and considerably strengthened it in 1245, and another Llywelyn besieged it—this time Llywelyn the Last, Prince of Wales. This siege of 1263 was long, but the Welsh were victorious and, for the last time, Deganwy Castle was demolished.

**Denbigh Castle,** *Denbigh, Denbighshire. South of town on Denbigh Hill off B4501.*

Before Denbigh Castle so prominently crowned

*Criccieth, on the Caernarvonshire coast; originally a stronghold of Llywelyn the Great, and for a time the prison of his recalcitrant son and grandson, it was later rebuilt and enlarged by Edward I*

73

the hill above the town, the town was known as the home of Dafydd ap Gruffydd, the fiery brother of Llywelyn, Prince of Wales. Exactly where his stronghold was built has never been determined, but although it was probably only a wooden tower on a motte it was certainly defensible, and it held out for some time against Edward I's forces during his conquest of Wales. Late in 1282 Denbigh, and Dafydd's stronghold, fell to the English, and the town and much surrounding country was granted to Henry de Lacy, Earl of Lincoln.

The Earl was commanded to build a castle and enclose the town, and no doubt the fine and extensive structure had already started to rise at the beginning of 1283. Apparently de Lacy's enthusiasm ran out when his only son was drowned in the castle well; he stopped work on the castle, and died not long after, in 1311. Before that, however, there was a revolt of the Welsh in the north, and documents refer to a significant Welsh victory at Denbigh in 1294. Whether or not this was the capture of the town and the castle or simply a battle victory is not clear, but the attempt to oust the English was soon put down.

After the death of the Earl of Lincoln, Denbigh changed hands a number of times, and many well known courtiers came to look on it as their headquarters. Among them was, apparently, Hugh le Despenser, favourite of Edward II, who had amassed so much territory—and such unpopularity —in the south. Then it was used by Roger Mortimer, favourite of Edward II's wife, Queen Isabella, Earl of March and architect of Edward's downfall. Many years later it was the headquarters of "Hotspur"—Henry Percy—and it was at this time that Owain Glyndwr's rising disrupted Wales and, in 1402, resulted in the burning of Denbigh town.

Just over 50 years later the Wars of the Roses began and Denbigh, like so many other strongholds, changed hands several times. In 1468, while it was being held by the Yorkists, it was besieged and eventually burnt by the king's half-brother, Jasper Tudor, Earl of Pembroke. The destruction caused this time was so great that the town was rebuilt on its present site, largely outside the town walls—which, judging by history, do not seem to have been very successful. The next notable owner of the castle was Dudley, Earl of Leicester and devoted favourite of Elizabeth I, who took possession

in 1563. He began to build Leicester's Chapel, intended to replace the Cathedral of St. Asaph, but died long before it could be finished, and now only a long wall near the castle entrance stands as a monument to this ambition.

A century later saw the outbreak of the Civil War, and Denbigh Castle was garrisoned for Charles I by a Colonel Salisbury. The king stayed in the castle for three days in 1645, after which the Great Kitchen Tower became known as the King's Chamber, or King Charles' Tower, doubtless because that was where he lodged. The town walls were defended at the same time as the castle, and were besieged by the Parliamentarians. Denbigh was one of the last to fall, and surrendered in 1646 to Major General Mytton, captor of Caernarvon and Conway Castles, the keys to the town and castle apparently being thrown down to him from Goblin Tower next to the castle. After the Restoration of 1660 Denbigh Castle was left deserted and was partly wrecked by gunpowder. The castle and the town walls deteriorated until the middle of the 19th Century, when considerable repairs were made. In 1920 care of the castle and the walls passed to the Government.

Edward I first had the town walls constructed to offer some immediate defence, and to guard the building of the castle. The castle itself was the second major step, and was placed in the highest, most inaccessible spot, the south-west corner. The outer walls of the castle are therefore continuations of the town wall, and are considerably thinner than the two inner walls. The outer castle walls were guarded by four large round towers, and the later inner walls by three great octagonal towers and by the main feature of the castle, the massive three-towered gatehouse to the town. This stage of building also included a great hall, cellars, and numerous chambers. A fairly modest barbican helped guard the formidable entrance, and at the south-east corner a postern was made in the outer wall. These outer walls had their defensive qualities increased by mantlets, or second screen walls, the southern mantlet which enclosed the postern and the two south towers being quite substantial, with a turret, and a barbican, part of it forming a very indirect path to the postern.

The castle and the town walls are badly ruined, though the wall boundary is still marked by stretches of high walls and the remains of towers, and the castle gatehouse is still imposing. The three towers were arranged so that a small octagonal courtyard was formed in the middle, and to reach it (where they would be exposed to fire from arrow slits on seven sides) assailants had to pass a drawbridge, two portcullises and two doors, and walk beneath a number of machicolations, or "murder holes". According to one old account, passages and dungeons to the east of the entrance were discovered and explored "to the extent of thirty yards", and in one was found the skeleton of a horse. These passages apparently linked the castle and the town. The same account relates that a walled-up chamber to the west of the entrance was discovered, in the 19th Century, to be full of gunpowder.

*Denbigh was a castle of Llywelyn's hot-headed brother Dafydd ap Gruffydd. Later castles on the site passed through the hands of several powerful barons including Roger Mortimer, Earl of March; "Harry Hotspur"; and Elizabeth's favourite Robert Dudley, Earl of Leicester*

**Dinas Powis Castle,** *St. Andrew's Major, Glamorgan. 4 miles south-west of Cardiff.*

A Welsh castle of two wards with masonry walls was built here, probably in the late 11th Century, on a site used for fortifications right back to the 5th or 6th Centuries A.D. In the inner ward there are the remains of a large round keep and a small round tower added in the 13th Century. Domestic buildings were put up a hundred years later, and the whole fortification was refitted a century after that. Documents indicate that it had a turbulent history, though few details are known. It was attacked in 1222, captured by Edward I's forces in 1277, retaken in 1287, captured back by the English in 1321, and attacked by Owain Glyndwr in 1403.

**Dinham Castle,** *Caerwent, Monmouthshire. 3½ miles west-south-west of Chepstow, between A48 and B4235.*

Dinham Castle presents numerous hints but little else. It is located on the side of a steep valley and has the remains of a rectangular tower which probably dates from the 13th Century. There are also the remains of various other rectangular constructions of uncertain character or purpose. It might be the place referred to in about 1150 as "Cestilldinam", but seems to have no other recorded history.

**Dolbadarn Castle,** *Llanberis, Caernarvonshire. 1 mile south-east of Llanberis off A4086, on edge Llyn Padarn.*

Dolbadarn was one of the royal castles of ancient Wales, and was built on a small rocky platform which drops very steeply on its east side 80 feet to Llyn Padarn, near its junction with Llyn Peris. With the fortifications at Deganwy, Harlech and Criccieth, and numerous other forts and camps, Dolbadarn turned Snowdonia into a vast mountainous stronghold, and it also guarded the main route from Caernarvon to the upper Vale of Con-

way, and central and Southern Wales. Although the early history of the castle and the site was never documented, some records suggest that Dolbadarn replaced Caernarvon as the seat of administration for the district of Arfon Is Gwyrfai, and it was possibly the stronghold of Welsh princes from the 6th Century A.D.

Whether the present site was the site of the earliest buildings will probably never be known, and even the present remains, rather than ancient records, have to hint at their own past. The round tower or keep now dominates the site, standing in part about 40 feet high, but it is some 100 years younger than the irregular, unmortared curtain wall which encloses the summit of the rock. One of the two rectangular towers in the curtain wall is probably the same age as the great round keep. But even the oldest part of the curtain wall is unlikely to have been built earlier than the second half of the 12th Century, and the round tower was almost certainly ordered by Llywelyn the Great, who used Dolbadarn frequently.

After the death of Llywelyn, and of his son six years later, the Welsh kingdom of Gwynedd became divided over the succession, and a rather restless unity was only achieved under Llywelyn ap Gruffydd, Prince of Wales, after he had defeated his rival claimants in 1255. One of his rivals had been his elder brother Owain Goch ("the Red"), and Llywelyn paid him back by imprisoning him in Dolbadarn Castle for twenty years—despite loud protests from the bards, who favoured Owain. But the Prince of Wales earned the wrath of Edward I, and within twelve years all Wales was under the English crown.

Dolbadarn Castle declined in importance after that, though Llywelyn's brother Dafydd used it as one of his strongholds. In Edward's second round of open warfare against the Welsh in 1282, Dolbadarn was captured by the Earl of Pembroke, and two years later it was partly dismantled by the king's forces, its timbers being taken to Caernarvon. From then on it must have deteriorated

*The ruins of Dolbadarn Castle, in a splendidly picturesque setting outside Llanberis. It was an ancient stronghold of Welsh chieftains, and fortification on this site may date back as far as the 6th Century*

rapidly, though there is a belief that Owain Glyndwr used the ruins as a prison during his rising of 1400—notably to hold Lord Grey of Ruthin to ransom (see Ruthin Castle). The site came under the guardianship of the Government in 1941, and the Department of the Environment has carried out site clearance and conservation.

**Dolforwyn Castle,** *Abermule, Montgomeryshire. 3½ miles north-east of Newtown off A483.*

Almost as an act of defiance to the English, Llywelyn the Last, Prince of Wales, built Dolforwyn Castle deep in the royal stronghold of Montgomeryshire. It was built on a ridge, and apparently the rectangular plan of the enclosure had no corner towers (there is now too little left of the castle to be certain about much of it). The single large round tower replaced a slightly earlier square tower, and it is possible the change was due to a change of mind rather than to the earlier tower being destroyed. All of the works seem to belong to the late 13th Century. After Edward's conquest of Wales and the death of Llywelyn in 1282, the Dolforwyn Castle was granted to Roger Mortimer.

**Dolwyddelan Castle,** *Dolwyddelan, Caernarvonshire. 5 miles south-west of Betwys-y-Coed on A496.*

Dolwyddelan Castle's fame is not in its structure, but in its prominence in the years between the ousting of the Normans and the crushing arrival of Edward I. (In fact only little is left of the structure —the ruin of a rectangular tower added to the castle in the 13th Century.) In Dolwyddelan Castle was born one of the immortal heroes of Wales— Llywelyn ap Iorwerth, "the Great", who gained recognition for Welsh rights in Magna Carta after

he joined the revolt of the barons against King John in 1215. He also established his supremacy over the other Welsh princes, and Dolwyddelan Castle was for many years his home.

The castle was founded by his father Iorwerth in about 1170, only a few years before Llywelyn was born. Dolwyddelan's ruins are on a rocky site which had a strong ditch defence. The ruined tower was not Llywelyn's birth place, being built a number of years after he died, and it must have replaced an earlier, weaker tower. Some experts argue that not even this site (at Nat. Grid Ref. SH 722523) was Iorwerth's castle, saying that the 12th Century castle traditionally sited at Dolwyddelan was really Tomen Castle on the rocky mound at SH 724521.

Dolwyddelan Castle was often used by Llywelyn's grandson, Llywelyn Prince of Wales, and in the same winter that the Prince was killed it fell to Edward I's forces.

**Domen Castell,** *Llanfechian, Montgomeryshire. 2½ miles east-north-east of Llanfyllin on B4393.*

One of the many sites of the early motte and bailey castles which used timber for their towers and walls. Now only earthworks remain, and the history of the site is unrecorded.

**Dryslwyn Castle,** *Dryslwyn, Carmarthenshire. 5 miles west of Llandeilo on B4297.*

All that remains of Dryslwyn Castle are the ruins of its chapel and hall—peaceful reminders of a far from peaceful past. The isolated hill the Welsh chose for their castle may once have borne a hill fort, but it is not now clear what sort of structure the princes of the south put up to command the region of Towy.

In the 13th Century Dryslwyn was held by Rhys ap Maredudd, a prince of the south who firmly resisted the growing power of the northern prince, Llywelyn ap Gruffydd (who became Prince of Wales). Rhys (grandson of the Lord Rhys—see Cilgerran Castle) allied himself with Edward I when the king crushed Llywelyn in the north in 1282; but instead of being given the power in Wales he had dreamed of, Rhys was put under jurisdiction of Edward's Justiciar and lost all his territories except Dryslwyn Castle. For Rhys that was a good deal worse than being overshadowed by Llywelyn, and in 1287 he raised a strong force of his former subjects for the same cause he had once betrayed—Welsh independence. Rhys achieved quick successes—he captured the castles at Dynevor, Carreg Cennen, and Llandovery, managed to avoid a relieving English force, and besieged Newcastle Emlyn, a former territory. The English succeeded in driving him from Emlyn, and Rhys escaped to Ireland. In 1290 he returned at the head of a very large but untrained army of Welsh peasants. This time Rhys was no match for the vengeful English. He was captured and taken to Edward at York. There he was dragged behind a horse to his death by beheading.

During Rhys's first rising, in 1287, Dryslwyn was besieged by the English as his only Welsh property, the siege being conducted by the Earl of Cornwall. The besiegers tried undermining one of the towers, but perhaps the props they used were too weak; the tunnel, and the tower above, collapsed while a large number of them—including Lord Stafford—were underground. None of those in the tunnel survived, but their comrades were able to capture the ruin. Some repairs must have been made during the following years, but Dryslwyn Castle's only other recorded part in national history was its brief capture by the Welsh under Owain Glyndwr in 1403.

**Dunraven Castle,** *Southerndown, Glamorgan. 5 miles south-west of Bridgend, off B4524.*

The old outbuildings and groves of trees do little to recall the long history of this site. (The last Dunraven Castle was not a true castle, but a 19th Century mansion topped by castellation, dismantled after the Second World War.) The area is supposed to have belonged to Caractacus before he was conquered by the Romans, but by the early 12th Century it definitely did belong to the Normans, and passed into the hands of Arnold de Boteler in return for his faithful service to its previous owner. It stayed in de Boteler's family for many generations, until marriage placed it under the Vaughans of Carmarthenshire.

The Vaughans were a large and powerful family, and it was only natural that there should have been an occasional black sheep among them. One or two of these apparently landed up at Dunraven in the 16th Century, and developed the habit of "wrecking" to bring in extra income. "Wrecking" involved showing lights on the coast during storms so that ships at sea would mistake them for a harbour or another ship's lights, sail on to the rocks and destroy themselves and their crews—leaving the wreckers to pick up the cargo the next morning. These Vaughans became highly expert at their grisly trade, and are even said to have hung lights on the horns of cattle to get realistic moving effects. The story goes that one night as Vaughan hurried down to see what ship he had snared, one of his men ran up to him carrying the severed hand of the ship's dead captain—and Vaughan saw by a ring on the hand that he had been responsible for the death of his own son. Horrified, Vaughan sold the estate, and in the early 19th Century it was acquired by the Dunravens.

**Dynevor Castle,** *Llandeilo, Carmarthenshire. 1 mile west of Llandeilo.*

The present Dynevor Castle was built in the last century, but the ruins of a 13th Century castle with frequent subsequent additions can still be seen on a site that is reputed to date back to A.D. 876 and Rhodri the Great. Rhodri had fortifications here, and on this spot decisions were taken which were to influence the history of Wales for hundreds of years. He divided the kingdom of Wales into three —Gwynedd (the north), Powis (central), and Deheubarth (south)—a division which unfortunately never did lead to greater peace.

The Welsh stronghold came into great prominence in the 11th Century, when Rhys ap Tewdwr rigidly

*Dolwydellan, birthplace and for many years
the home of Llywelyn the Great, who secured
many advantages for his countrymen by
joining the English barons in revolt against
King John*

held it—and so many other parts of Wales—
against the Norman invaders, and Dynevor continued as one of the seats of the princes of South
Wales. In 1287 another Rhys captured the castle
from the English after Edward's Welsh campaigns
(see Dryslwyn Castle); in fact, practically every
occupier in the intervening centuries was also
named Rhys. Tradition does not identify the Rhys
of Dynevor who is said to have imprisoned his
father and brother in the castle, to ensure that he
inherited the riches he coveted. For extra security
he had his brother's eyes put out; but the blind
man knew the castle so well that he was able to feel
his way to his father's cell and release him.

The castle that the first Lord Rhys occupied was
dismantled in 1220, but the late 12th Century
wards are traceable. A large round keep was added
in the 13th Century after the destruction of 1220,
as was a small round tower. Domestic buildings

date from over one hundred years later, and much
refurbishing was apparently carried out at the turn
of the 15th and 16th Centuries. Owain Glyndwr
nearly repeated Rhys ap Maredudd's success, and
caused much damage to the castle in 1403, though
he could not capture it.

**Dyserth Castle,** *Dyserth, Flintshire. $3\frac{1}{2}$ miles east-
south-east of Rhyl.*

The beginnings of this modest-sized English castle
are a little confused—and it is also sometimes
known as Caerfaelan, Carregfaelan, Castle of the
Rock, and Castle de Rupe. A castle was perhaps
begun very close to the present site in 1238, but the
position chosen of the structure must have been
unsuitable, for another castle was built (or the first
rebuilt) in 1241. However it started, the castle was
attacked by the Welsh in 1245, and its short confused career came to an end less than twenty years
later when it was destroyed in another attack.

**Ednyfed's Castle,** *Rhos on Sea, Denbighshire. $1\frac{1}{4}$
miles north-west of Colwyn Bay off A546.*

The nearby Parish Church houses the tomb of
Ednyfed who founded a castle on the site in the
13th Century. A manor house was built over the
old castle's remains two hundred years later, and
it is the ivy covered ruin of this which can be seen
today.

**Ewloe Castle,** *Ewloe, Flintshire. 10 miles south-east
of Holywell on A55.*

The eventual insignificance of Ewloe Castle after
the building of the giants of Rhuddlan and Flint
has preserved its ruins in reasonable condition, and
this and its association with the greatest Welsh
names rescue it from obscurity. The castle and its
district fall to the east of Offa's Dyke, once the
boundary between the two countries, which ex-

plains the very English name. Ewloe became Welsh after the victories of Owain Gwynedd in the north, and the capture of Mold in 1146 was doubtless soon followed by a simple Welsh castle—probably a motte and bailey type—on the present site. The existing D-shaped keep, called the Welsh Tower, was built soon after 1200.

Llywelyn ap Iorwerth (Llywelyn the Great) took away the Gwynedd territory from Owain's son, and held Ewloe Castle until he died in 1240. After his death the Welsh again became disunited, and the English recovered much of North-East Wales. It was not until Llywelyn's grandson, Llywelyn ap Gruffydd, established his superiority and took back the border areas, that Ewloe Castle was once again in Welsh hands. This Llywelyn, who became Prince of Wales, made considerable additions to the castle in and shortly after 1257, adding a stronger curtain around the Welsh Tower, and

building a second ward down the slope with a round tower at its furthest extremity.

But then came Edward I, and the loss of so many of Llywelyn's possessions. A very large earth mound south (and uphill) of the upper ward can still be seen, and it is quite likely that this was built by Edward's forces to help besiege Llywelyn's castle, as its threatening positioning makes it unlikely to be a Welsh work. By 1277 Llywelyn had to settle peace terms with Edward, who then began his castle at nearby Flint, which made Ewloe militarily unimportant from then on.

*Ewloe Castle, a border stronghold which changed hands several times between Welsh and English in the 12th and 13th Centuries.*
*Opposite: Flint Castle, established by Edward I in 1277–80. The Donjon or Great Tower has walls up to 23 feet thick*

# F

built with the greatest urgency. Within a month, the equivalent of almost £100,000 had been spent and 950 men were employed in the first week on the ditches and various earthwork defences. Edward started to put into practice his habit (learnt in France) of establishing defended towns at the same time as castles.

Much of the castle's original extent is badly ruined, for it had a large but weak outer bailey. The square inner bailey, however, still shows three corner towers and the huge Great Tower, or Donjon of the castle. This was slightly apart from the walls of the inner bailey, and defended by its own moat and drawbridge, resembling nothing so much as a traditional and extremely strong round keep— though it was apparently never completely finished. The Donjon must have been the focus of the castle —it had a chapel and a variety of other rooms, and with walls 23 feet thick at the base it must have

**Flint Castle,** *Flint, Flintshire. North of town near coast.*

After he had overpowered Llywelyn, Prince of Wales, and stripped him of his power and his territories in the bitter treaty at Rhuddlan, Edward wasted no time in establishing his superiority on a permanent basis, and in the summer of 1277 ordered the building of a castle in Flint. This was

been impregnable. Work on the castle seems to have stopped in 1280, but in 1282 Llywelyn followed his brother Dafydd in rebelling against the king, and Flint Castle was fiercely attacked by the Welsh, parts of it falling into their hands. But it did not take Edward long to overcome the Welsh again, and Flint was once more secure.

Two of England's most tragic kings later had cause to remember Flint Castle. Edward II welcomed Piers Gaveston, his much-banished favourite, to Flint Castle in 1311; and in 1399 Richard II, tricked by the Earl of Northumberland into leaving Wales for London to meet Henry Bolingbroke, Duke of Lancaster, was ambushed, escorted to Flint Castle, and persuaded to abdicate in favour of Henry (see Conway Castle). Not surprisingly, there is a colourful account about this stage of the deserted king's downfall, concerning Richard's faithful bloodhound Math. Math had always refused to go with anyone but Richard, and would scarcely leave his side. But while Richard and Henry were talking in the courtyard of Flint Castle, Math, untied by a servant, ran this time to Henry, showing him all the affection he had previously kept for Richard. Richard took this (correctly) to be symbolic, and the account relates that Math never again followed Richard, who shortly thereafter lost his crown.

**Fonmon Castle,** *Penmark, Glamorgan. 4 miles west of Barry.*

Parts of a 13th and 14th Century castle, comprising two round towers and a rectangular one which may have been the keep, are retained in the structure of a much more modern house. The castle seems to have no recorded history.

G

**Grosmont Castle,** *Grosmont, Monmouthshire. 9 miles north-east of Abergavenny on B4347.*

A short distance from the point where the Golden Valley joins the Monmow river stand the remains of Grosmont Castle, which once guarded the Golden Valley with Skenfrith Castle and White Castle, strengthening the Norman hold on the district of Abergavenny and keeping the Welsh away from the English plains. All that is left of Grosmont Castle now are the ruins of the inner ward gateway, part of the central hall, and two round towers on the enclosing wall—testimony to a turbulent past. Even these remains show that the castle was once very important, and that it had been finely executed—the 13th Century octagonal chimney of the hall being a striking feature.

The ruins are of mixed dates—the hall block is early 13th Century and seems to have been part of a rebuilding operation carried out under King John, or Henry III. Considerable work is supposed to have been done in 1201 by Hubert de Burgh, but the Pipe Roll mentions it as early as 1163, and it is quite likely that some fortification existed soon after the Norman advances of around 1070. In the mid-13th Century the hall block (which perhaps served as a keep) was enclosed with three round towers and the gatehouse, but alterations at the beginning of the next century removed one of the towers.

Henry III came to Grosmont Castle with his queen after Llywelyn the Great had stirred up so much unrest in Wales, and won the support of a number of the Border Lords. The royal presence certainly did not deter the Welsh leader, however, who in a surprise night attack captured the castle and forced Henry, his wife and their retinue to flee into the darkness. Another Welsh bid for independence was less successful here. Owain

Glyndwr's revolt put Rhys Gethin in the castle, but Henry of Monmouth (who became Henry V) easily ousted him in 1410, in one of the last defeats needed to convince Glyndwr of the hopelessness of his attempt.

*Grosmont Castle, one of the English border castles guarding the Golden Valley. A night attack by the followers of Llywelyn the Great forced King Henry III to flee, just in time to avoid capture with the garrison*

**Gwrych Castle,** *Abergele, Denbighshire. 1 mile west of Abergele off A55.*

One of the most striking and picturesque residences in Wales, Gwrych is not, despite its name and appearance, a true castle, and several of the impressive towers are sham. It was not built until 1815, and it was once the home of the Earl of Dundonald, the famous soldier of the South African War. Although the castle was not there to see them, historic events which are supposed to have taken place in the locality are recorded on tablets at the castle gateway—including the ambush of Richard II after he was deceived into leaving Conway Castle by the Earl of Northumberland.

**Gwydir Castle,** *Llanrwst (Denbighshire), Caernarvonshire. Across Conway river on Caernarvonshire side of Llanrwst.*

The present mansion was rebuilt in 1920 after it had been gutted by fire, the original buildings dating from 1555. Now it is a dignified Tudor-style mansion in fine gardens which are also occupied by a number of magnificent peacocks.

**Harlech Castle,** *Harlech, Merioneth. On edge of town, on A496.*

When Harlech Castle was built the sea was half a mile closer, and swept into a harbour that clung to the foot of the towering crag on which the fortress was founded. Thus the castle, with its massive eastern towers and enormous twin-towered gatehouse facing inland, and its comparatively weaker back defended by the sea like an endless moat, owes much of its power to its site. For that reason (although there is no conclusive evidence either way) it is easy to believe that the site had always been sought after: that an early Welsh fort called Caer Collwyn did stand there, and that the ancient legend that this was the home of Bran the Blessed and Bronwen of the White Neck is not legend but fact. (This legend also told of Bronwen being buried at Amlwch in Anglesey, and a mound excavated there did reveal an Iron Age urn filled with cremated bones.)

Whatever its previous history, the meticulous records of the English kings ensured that the site was documented when the victorious forces of Edward I arrived at Harlech with a large number of masons and quarrymen in 1283, preparing to make certain that no more Llewelyns would rise to threaten the sovereignty of England. The growing town was visited by Edward twice during the following year, though little of the construction was then under way. Even in 1285 the major work undertaken seems to have been the moat cut into the rock in front of the castle site, but then things speeded up and over 850 men were employed during the next two summers. By 1290 Harlech Castle was all but finished, having taken longer than Conway to build, but at a cost of less than half that spent on that most expensive town defence system.

The design of the concentric Harlech Castle was largely entrusted to the King's master mason, James of St. George, the military engineer whose skills are reflected in every Edwardian castle in Wales, and quite a number besides (the engineer was also made constable of Harlech Castle from 1290–93). The inner walls of the strongest part, the east front, were built nine to twelve feet thick, and though the three other inner walls were initially considerably thinner, they were soon thickened and strengthened, as were the walls of the western towers, the two turreted round towers commanding the precipitous slope to the sea. Dominating the whole castle, and today still the most awesome sight at Harlech, was the twin-towered gatehouse. A gatehouse on such a scale was more than simply that, and had more in common with the older keeps as a place for a self-contained, last ditch stand. But it was designed with comfort and practicality in mind as well, as it contained the rooms of the constable of the castle. The entrance way was guarded by a number of portcullises and doors, and by no fewer than seven "murder holes". The outer bailey of the castle was made very narrow, with a low curtain, since the castle proper takes up almost the whole of the site.

Harlech Castle's defences were first put to the test in 1294, when it was besieged during Madoc's uprising—a test it passed easily, though with important help from the sea, provisions for the 37-strong garrison coming by ship from Conway and Caernarvon to the tiny harbour 200 feet below the castle walls. After Madoc's vain rebellion Edward used Harlech to imprison captives from his campaign in Scotland, but like the bigger castles of

*Opposite: one of the peacocks of Gwydir Castle, a relatively new building on the site of an Elizabethan mansion*

Caernarvon and Conway it began to fall into disuse and neglect. In the early 14th Century many repairs were made—particularly to the roofs; and by 1343 the chapel was noted as being "weak and ruinous".

A much grimmer test came in the next major Welsh rising—the long and temporarily successful revolt led by Owain Glyndwr in 1400. Early in the campaign Harlech Castle was besieged, it being a relatively simple task to cut off the castle from the routes to other English strongholds. Six miles away across Tremadoc Bay, Criccieth Castle was also to undergo siege, and this time neither of the castles could look forward to relief from the sea, for Owain Glyndwr had the support of the French and a French fleet was in the Irish Sea. The siege of Harlech Castle was long and grim. The garrison of some 40 men grew mutinous under the harrowing conditions, some (including the constable) wanting to surrender. The diehards resisted and kept back the would-be capitulators. The last hope for Harlech and Criccieth, early in 1404, lay with a messenger sent from Criccieth to get help from Conway. When his mission failed the fight went out of Harlech, and Owain Glyndwr reached the highest stage of his rebellion. He made Harlech his capital and held at least one parliament in the castle. Brilliant as his revolt may have been, it could not be sustained against the vengeance of the English and the apathy of many Welshmen; in 1409 a force of 1,000, in part led by John Talbot (later the antagonist of Joan of Arc), got through to Harlech and recovered the castle. Glyndwr's wife, their daughter, and four grandchildren were taken prisoner (Glyndwr himself having fled), and Wales' bid for freedom was almost over.

Harlech—and most of Wales—only enjoyed another fifty years of uneasy peace before it was rocked by the Wars of the Roses, and after Henry VI was defeated and captured in the summer of 1460 at Northampton, his wife Margaret of Anjou took shelter at Harlech Castle before going to Scotland to raise forces against the Yorkists. The town had been made a headquarters by Henry's half-brother, Jasper Tudor, and the constable of the castle, Dafydd ap Ieuan, was also a staunch Lancastrian. Once again Harlech was fiercely besieged—this time by the Yorkists led by Lord Herbert, Earl of Pembroke, and his brother Sir Richard Herbert—and the famous marching song "The Men of Harlech" was inspired by the hardships endured by the garrison. Dafydd held out well after other Lancastrian commanders in England and Wales had surrendered to the Yorkists, and widened his fame by replying to one summons to surrender with the boast that he had once held a castle in France so long against siege that all the old women in Wales talked of it; and now he would hold a castle in Wales until the old women of France talked of it. But eventually famine was once again the victor, and Dafydd surrendered to the Herberts on honourable terms. The Yorkists were so impressed by the Harlech garrison's bravery that when Edward IV at first refused to honour the terms of the settlement, Sir Richard Herbert apparently promised the king that he would put Dafydd and his garrison back in the castle, and let the king try to get them out—also offering his own life in exchange for Dafydd's, rather than see his promise broken.

Like so many other castles after the Wars of the Roses, Harlech became a pointless structure; it decayed rapidly until only the north-east, or Prison Tower, had a roof, and that was only because the tower was still used as a debtor's prison. With all the neglect, it is surprising that 200 years later it was able to endure yet another long siege. When the Civil War began in 1642 Harlech was held for Charles I by Sir Hugh Pennant, and later by Colonel William Owen, against the Parliamentarians. Once again Harlech was the last to surrender (in the first part of the Civil War), its garrison of 50 not giving in to the ubiquitous Major-General Mytton until March 1647. Fortunately for the garrison as well as for the thousands who are awed each summer by the ruins, Cromwell's forces had been prevented by bad roads from bringing their artillery to Harlech; equally fortunately, Parliamentary orders for Harlech's demolition were never carried out.

The decay was stopped in 1914 when care of the castle passed to the Government, and the post of constable of Harlech Castle is now normally held by the Lord Lieutenant of Merioneth. Although the sea has retreated the setting is still striking, and it is clear why famine was the only consistent conqueror. The restorative work gives a visitor many opportunities to recall the castle's turbulent

past, marvel at the gatehouse, and enjoy the superb
views from the wall walks.

*The gatehouse, Harlech Castle*

**Halkyn Castle,** *Halkyn, Flintshire. 3½ miles south-south-east of Holywell off A55.*

A mansion that was once one of the seats of the Duke of Westminster, who built a beautiful church near the estate's entrance lodge.

**Haverfordwest Castle,** *Haverfordwest, Pembrokeshire. On east side of town.*

The shell of a castle on a strong rocky site above the Western Cleddau dates mostly from the 13th Century, and was built by William de Valence. It is quite likely that the site was used well before

that; one source asserts that Gilbert de Clare built a castle there early in the 12th Century, and that the whole town, but not the castle, was burnt in 1220 by Llywelyn the Great. The town suffered an identical fate much later, with the castle again standing undefeated above the flames. Again it was a patriot Welshman who led the attacking forces—Owain Glyndwr, in 1405.

A sad legend associated with Haverfordwest Castle depends on a Norman castle having been built there, for it tells of the cruelty suffered at Norman hands by an imprisoned Welsh raider. However the governor's young son had been attracted by the Welshman's alleged bowmanship and notoriety and eventually the two met every day, the prisoner telling the governor's child many exciting stories of battle and adventure. But the hunger for vengeance still burned deep in the Welshman and one day he took the boy to the top of the castle tower. Despite the pleadings and promises of governor, the prisoner threw the child from the tower and then leapt to his own death. The grieving father set up a monastery in memory of his child, and named it "Sorrowful".

There was nothing triumphant about the events at Haverfordwest during the Civil War. It was garrisoned for Charles I, but there was no chance for the Parliamentarians to besiege it, since the Royalist garrison fled when they heard of their colleagues' defeat at Milford. When the Parliamentarian army commanders who had won that battle and had occupied Pembroke suddenly turned against him and went to the Royalist side, Cromwell ordered the destruction of Haverfordwest Castle in case the same should happen there. That must have been no easy task—Cromwell ordered the townspeople themselves to do it, and there are documents which record the requests of the town leaders for more and more money to pay the citizens, more men from outside, gunpowder, and equipment. At least the destruction was not total, and now the ruins are a dominating landmark.

*Haverfordwest Castle: on two occasions—in 1220 and 1405—the town was burnt out by Welsh attackers, but the castle survived each time*

**Hawarden Old Castle,** *Hawarden, Flintshire. 10 miles south-east of Holywell on A55.*

In the grounds of a large park are the ruins of the "Old Castle", as it is locally called; part of the banqueting hall, and the original huge round keep with its well-preserved chapel are the main features. In the late 13th Century a small round tower was added, and later still came a complex structure, and the large square hall tower.

The early history is obscure; it was attacked by the Welsh in a border struggle in 1205, and was in Welsh hands during 1267. Following the victory of Edward I ten years later and the building of Flint Castle, Hawarden Castle reverted to English ownership. During Edward's second suppression of the Welsh under Llywelyn, Prince of Wales, on the night of Palm Sunday 1282, in the midst of a torrential storm, Llywelyn's brother Dafydd and his followers stormed the castle and captured it.

Garrisoned for Charles I in the Civil War, Hawarden Castle fell to the Parliamentarians more by betrayal than by siege, but was retaken by the Royalists, before Parliamentary victories in the area forced it to change hands yet again. Four years later, in 1647, Cromwell ordered it to be slighted. The style "Old" came with the building of a mansion in 1752. It was here that Gladstone, the Victorian politician, married the heiress, Catherine Glynne, in 1839, and it was his home for 60 years.

**Hay Castle,** *Hay-on-Wye, Breconshire. In town, 14 miles north-east of Brecon on A438.*

The first Norman in these parts was a knight named Revell, and as he was one of Henry I's men the motte and bailey castle he established was probably begun very soon after Henry came to the throne in 1100. A castle at Hay was mentioned in documents of 1121, and while it is likely that this was Revell's castle, the site referred to was probably not the site of the present remains (at Nat. Grid Ref. SO 229423) but the nearby trace of a motte (at SO 226422). What is left now, and known as Hay Castle, is mainly a length of walling and a 13th Century gateway which adjoins the newer residential quarters built during the reign of Elizabeth I (1533–1603) and which are privately owned.

*Hawarden Old Castle, captured in a night attack under cover of a storm in 1282 by Dafydd, brother of the Prince of Wales*

The ruins therefore date from considerably later than the first Norman castle, and they must have been built by King John after he captured and burnt the original fortress in 1216. The building was apparently carried out under the direction and supervision of one of the most reviled and treacherous Marcher Lords, William de Braose. There is also an old tradition that it was William's wife,

Maude de Valerie, who built the castle—and literally built it, with her own hands. However true this is, she must have been a formidable and strong-minded woman, for among all the aristocracy she alone accused King John of murdering his nephew, Prince Arthur. In return for this courage, or foolhardiness, Maud was thrown into prison at Corfe Castle, where she eventually starved to death.

Nothing remarkable seems to have happened at the castle for almost two hundred years, though it apparently changed hands briefly in 1231 and again in 1265. Owain Glyndwr caused considerable damage to both the town and the castle in 1400, in the early days of his rising against Henry IV, but Hay Castle was listed as defensible in 1403, and nothing seems to have been heard of it after that.

**Hen Blas Castle,** *Flint, Flintshire. 1¼ miles north-west of Flint, between A548 and A55.*

At the intersection of two steep valleys is the site of a castle which shows, by the earthworks which remain, that it once had an inner ward and a large outer enclosure, a formation perhaps developed from a very early motte and bailey castle. Its history is unknown, but in 1244 a wooden castle was documented as being "at Coleshill" which is less than half a mile away. There are also traces of a stone structure from the 13th or 14th Century, but it has been established that these had no military purpose.

**Hen Castell,** *Llangattock, Breconshire. 1¼ miles south of Crickhowell off A40.*

With no recorded history, and the masonry almost completely disappeared, the original character and purpose of Hen Castell is difficult even to guess at. The site is on a hillside, and a ditch—probably a moat—completely surrounds the square platform which projects from the slope, its sides revetted in stone.

**Hên Castle,** *Saundersfoot, Pembrokeshire. 3½ miles north of Tenby, off B4316.*

Hên is the Welsh for "old", and is pronounced *hayne*. Sometimes, especially in the local area, where its wooded park borders the village, it is written "Hean" Castle. This disputed name seems to be all that is known about the site.

**Holt Castle,** *Holt, Denbighshire. 5 miles north-east of Wrexham on A534.*

The strategic position occupied by Holt on the Wales/England border made it an important castle in the 13th Century, but it was probably also important for hundreds of years before that. Bronze Age remains have been found on the site, and the castle may occupy the same site which once bore the Roman fort of Bovium. (This was a supply station for the large fort at Chester, and was also part of the communication line with the south.) The compact and powerful Edwardian castle was built by the Earl of Surrey, John de Warenne, near the end of the 13th Century. It had a pentagonal plan, with round angle-towers built outside, against an isolated boss of rock. Now only the rock and some stonework survive. Like many castles, Holt changed hands at least twice during the 1642–1647 Civil War, but little else is known of its history.

K

**Keeston Castle,** *Keeston, Pembrokeshire. 4 miles north-west of Haverfordwest off A487.*

This is often stated as being a true castle site, but some experts are equally adamant that it has never had anything to do with a castle.

**Kenfig Castle,** *Kenfig, Glamorganshire. 5 miles south-south-west of Port Talbot off B4283.*

The sad and mysterious ruins of Kenfig Castle have now almost vanished. It was once (according to excavations in 1927) a castle with a very substantial square keep built over a large vaulted basement which was covered with earth to practically form a motte. This was built in the 12th Century by Robert, Earl of Gloucester, and a town soon flourished alongside. In the 13th Century and the early 14th, a "chemise", or narrow wall, was built around the keep, and a large bailey with a gatehouse probably enclosed the whole town. This must have been after 1232, for in an attack of that date it was noted that the only masonry was the tower keep (records of 1185 mention wood being taken to Kenfig Castle). The castle was referred to again in 1295 as being recently burnt, and it was captured during a local uprising in 1321.

In fact an enemy more powerful than Welsh rebels, and more powerful than all the Kings of England, was already attacking Kenfig Castle, for the sand dunes were creeping steadily inland. The castle and its hamlet doubtless struggled on for many years; but early in the 16th Century a storm of great violence speeded up the process, and almost overnight the dunes smothered the last houses and walls. Now all that is left are a few ruins near the railway line, the records of the excavation of 1927, and a legend which says that beneath Kenfig Pool, a freshwater pool on the edge of the dunes, lies the true city of Kenfig. It is said that on a clear, still day roofs and chimneys can be seen in the depths— and when the wind ripples the water, a watery bell tolls its lament.

**Kidwelly Castle,** *Kidwelly, Carmarthenshire. 8 miles south of Carmarthen on A484.*

In its early years Kidwelly Castle was so often occupied by the Welsh that a glance at that period of its history almost suggests it must have been a Welsh castle. In fact the first castle on the rocky site above the mouth of the Gwendraeth Fach was built by Roger, Bishop of Salisbury, one of the Norman King Henry I's ministers. It must have been begun very early in the 12th Century, for there was a mention of the castle's hall in 1114. That castle was one of a line of castles along the coastal road that was built during the Norman advance throughout Henry's reign, but after his death Wales began to unite against the invaders, and in 1136 the battle of Maes Gwenllian was fought near Kidwelly. The Welsh were led by Gwenllian, wife of Gryffydd ap Rhys, and the Normans by the Lord of Kidwelly, Maurice de Londres, and by the Bishop's constable. The Normans won, and Gwenllian and her son were captured and killed. She naturally became a heroine, and is remembered by the name of the battle and its site, "maes" being Welsh for "field of". Maurice de Londres at that time also owned Ogmore in Glamorgan, and when Bishop Roger died he seems to have taken over Kidwelly as well. Apart from the semi-circular moat and the rampart under the outer curtain which still survives, little is known about the structure of the first small castle, as it was completely covered by the late 13th Century and early 14th Century work. The castle was frequently under attack, and was captured by the Welsh many times—so much so that old Welsh chronicles report that the Lord Rhys "built" Kidwelly castle in 1190. This must have been a way of recording Rhys's occupation and repair of the castle, for by 1201 the Normans were back in it and in that year Rhys's son Meredith died at the hands of the garrison during another bid to capture the castle. Another of Rhys's sons, Rhys Grug, took revenge in 1215 when he burnt and captured Kidwelly, holding it for seven years until Llewelyn the Great forced him to return it to the English as part of his plan to win acceptance for Wales. The heiress to Kidwelly, at this time, was Hawise de Londres who married into the powerful Marcher Lord family of de Braose; but her husband died in a campaign in 1233, by which time Kidwelly Castle was once again firmly in Welsh hands, and had been for two years, Llewelyn having decided that appeasement would not work with Henry III. The Welsh hung on to Kidwelly for a long time,

and only after Hawise married Patrick de Chaworth in 1244 did she find someone to get her
castle back for her. De Chaworth even managed to
hold Kidwelly Castle during the Welsh rising of
1257, though the town of Kidwelly was destroyed.
But the next year Patrick was killed in battle, and
his estate went to his son Payn, who began considerable rebuilding after his majority in about
1270. The curtain and four angle towers of the
inner ward were built by Payn; he died in 1279, five
years after his long-suffering mother, Hawise, and
four years before his brother Patrick—whose infant daughter Matilda then inherited the estate.
Edward I arranged that Matilda should marry
Henry, son of the king's brother Edmund, Earl of
Lancaster, and in 1291 Henry of Lancaster became
the lord of Kidwelly Castle. The next major stages
of construction took place under Henry—first a
chapel and new domestic buildings in the inner
ward, and then, to bring the castle fully up-to-date
with the concentric pattern displayed by Caerphilly, Harlech, and Beaumaris, an outer curtain
with a massive gatehouse, a smaller one, and four
round towers. Except for a brief period when
Edward II confiscated them, the estates stayed in
Lancastrian hands, passing to John of Gaunt, later

*Kidwelly, a Norman castle which was in*
*Welsh hands for many years in the 12th and*
*13th Centuries. It later passed to the Crown*

the Duke of Lancaster, when the inheritance
passed from Matilda to her sister Blanche de
Chaworth, who by then was married to John of
Gaunt. Later Kidwelly's importance faded considerably, especially after it became Crown property on the accession of Henry IV in 1399. Henry
VII granted it to Sir Rhys ap Tewdwr, but his
grandson forfeited it in 1531. Eventually Kidwelly
Castle passed to the Earls of Cawdor, to whom it
still belongs, guardianship now being with the
Department of Environment.
Many repairs and careful strengthening have made
Kidwelly the best preserved of the Carmarthenshire castles, and it presents an impressive sight
above the plains of the Gwendraeth Fach. The
main gatehouse is excellently preserved (although
begun in the early 14th Century, it was almost completely rebuilt between 1388 and 1422), and the
four 13th Century towers of the inner courtyard
can be climbed. The domestic arrangements can be
followed clearly, and the 14th Century chapel is
unusually well preserved. (It is also worth pointing

out that the "ll" in Kidwelly is pronounced like an English "l", perhaps a unique occurrence among Welsh names.)

**Knighton Castle,** *Knighton, Radnorshire. On south, upper end of town, 15 miles east-north-east of Llandrindod Wells off A488.*

There are very scanty traces of the castle that watched over Knighton (and which perhaps gave the nearby mound its name of Bryn-y-Castell), but it was a timber and earthwork castle which seems never to have been reinforced with stone, so it probably vanished centuries ago. It is possible that Knighton had a strong wall in 1402, but all trace of this, too, has disappeared.

*Laugharne Castle: the old castle, much fought over in the 12th and 13th Centuries, was incorporated into a Tudor mansion*

**Knucklas Castle,** *Knucklas, Radnorshire. 3 miles north-west of Knighton on B4355.*

The castle is also sometimes called Conoclas Castle, and derives its name from y Cnwclas, which means "the green hillock"; and briefly in the 13th Century the castle did crown the green "hillock" on which very little of its remains can be seen today. The site is a strong one, and "hillock" does not do it justice, for one side is a high, steep cliff. There are signs that there were several enclosures and at its height it was probably a square masonry enclosure with four round towers. Before that it may have been a hill fort, while local tradition claims it as their site for King Arthur's marriage to Guinevere. The castle's recorded history is brief and obscure. The first mention of it in chronicles is in 1246 and its capture in 1262 may have been the end of it since it was not listed among the castles which Mortimer seized in 1322. Nor does it figure in the review of castles in the war preparations of 1403, and three years later the lordship was treated as having no castle.

# L

**Laugharne Castle,** *Laugharne, Carmarthenshire. On foreshore 9 miles south-west of Carmarthen on A4066.*

Laugharne Castle, like border fortifications everywhere, has a history of constantly changing possession. In its early days (a mention in a document of 1116 possibly refers to this castle) it was repeatedly taken by the Welsh and wrecked, and repeatedly won back by the Normans. It was still changing hands into the second half of the 13th Century, and its first well-established ownership was probably that of Sir Guy de Brian in the early 14th Century. Laugharne was listed as defensible in 1403.

Its original form is uncertain, as the old castle was incorporated into the reconstruction, as a mansion, of some of the buildings by Sir John Perrot during the reign of Henry VIII. The medieval remains consist mainly of an early round keep, and a round tower which was probably built near the end of the 13th Century. The ruins of the gatehouse are also quite well preserved, and this dates from soon after the tower.

**Llanblethian Castle,** *Llanblethian, Glamorgan. $\frac{1}{2}$ mile south-west of Cowbridge.*

Llanblethian Castle is also popularly known as St. Quintin's Castle, after the St. Quintin family, but they did not own it until much later than the 14th Century when the castle was begun; the first mention of it, as being recently begun, is in a document of 1314. It is likely that some fortification, and perhaps a castle, existed here well before that date, for in the middle of the ruins is what may be the trace of a keep. The traceable features show that it was a castle with one ward, a square tower and two round ones, and a very fine twin-towered gatehouse which is now the main feature of the castle. Where work can be dated, the date is the 14th Century, and an earlier castle must remain conjecture, although the town of Cowbridge was founded because of the proximity of Llanblethian. The lordship of Llanblethian was already a borough before the 14th Century, and the settlement itself goes back to Roman times.

**Llandaff Castle,** *Llandaff, Glamorgan. In north-west area of Cardiff.*

There is apparently no recorded history of this castle, although according to tradition it was burnt by Owain Glyndwr when his revolt spread to the south at the beginning of the 15th Century. The main feature of the ruins is the twin-towered gatehouse, probably dating from the early 14th Century. The castle was small, and its four irregular sides were guarded by three small towers, one round, one square, and another which has vanished.

**Llanddew Castle,** *Llanddew, Breconshire. 1½ miles north-north-east of Brecon.*

The 1347 Register of Edward, Prince of Wales (the Black Prince) mentions Llanddew Castle, but that is all that seems to be known of this walled enclosure whose domestic buildings were apparently guarded by only one small, squat round tower.

**Llandovery Castle,** *Llandovery, Carmarthenshire. In grounds of Castle Hotel on south edge of town.*

The Norman castle established by Richard Fitz Pons, which once dominated the district, was captured by the Welsh in 1116 almost before the mortar had dried, and held until the English won it back in 1272. Now only the shattered remains of the keep are left—not surprisingly, for after its capture from the Welsh it changed hands again four times in the next fifteen years, and was attacked by Owain Glyndwr's rebels in 1403.

**Llanfair Discoed Castle,** *Llanfair Discoed, Monmouthshire. 9½ miles east-north-east of Newport.*

Later additions have obscured much of an early or mid-13th Century castle, but two round towers and part of the gatehouse remain. It apparently has no recorded history.

**Llangathen Castle,** *Llangathen, Carmarthenshire. 3½ miles west of Llandeilo.*

Lord Rhys is said to have built this small castle, now badly ruined, at the time that he held Carreg Cennen Castle as part of the inheritance of Dynevor in the last part of the 12th Century. Nothing seems to have been recorded of its history.

**Llangibby Castle,** *Llangybi, Monmouthshire. 7 miles north-north-east of Newport off A449.*

Also sometimes called Castell Tregrug, these ruins stand on a large summit site. Llangibby was an unusual castle—it has only one ward, but it is exceptionally large, and the very elongated keep was a curious choice. The huge gatehouse could have been individually defensible, like the keep, and there are the remains of three towers, though probably four existed originally. A turret and a smaller gatehouse can also be traced. All the work points to the early 14th Century, though documents mention it as a stone structure in 1286. However, it could be that there was an earlier earthwork castle on the site, or very near to it, which also had its masonry removed for the new castle. At any rate, it seems that Llangibby Castle was never finished.

**Llangynwyd Castle,** *Llangynwyd, Glamorgan. 1½ miles south of Maesteg.*

This 13th Century castle's history came to an end before the century itself, for there is no record of it after a mention of it being burnt in 1295. It is now very much ruined, but the earthworks were once strong, with a double-towered gatehouse and at least one large tower.

**Llanmaes Castle,** *Llanmaes, Glamorgan. 8 miles west of Barry.*

There is apparently no record of Llanmaes Castle's history, nor why it should have the alternative names of Bedford Castle or Malefunt Castle. All that is left are the featureless remains of a corner of a square tower.

**Llanquian Castle,** *Cowbridge, Glamorgan. 10 miles west of Cardiff.*

Fragmentary remains of a motte and bailey castle in which the main masonry was probably the revetting of a natural knoll or a motte. It seems to have no known history.

**Llanstephan Castle,** *Llanstephan, Carmarthenshire. 7½ miles south-south-west of Carmarthen, off B4312.*

High on a bluff fronting the sea, on a small peninsula formed by the Gwendraeth, Towy, and Taf rivers, are the striking ruins of Llanstephan Castle, which have caught the attention of many Romantic painters. It is also a unique castle, for while it was never one of the most important, its structure is unlike any other. It must also have had a longer and more complex roll of owners than practically any other castle.

The site the castle occupies is a strong one—only from the west is an approach not prevented by steep drops to the water. It was probably appreciated long before medieval times, for a strong bank and ditch west of the castle was most likely the bulwark of an Iron Age fort. Further powerful earthworks were built to form the oval Upper Ward and a large outer bailey—the Lower Ward—but eventually stone walls enclosed the whole area, with no separation between the wards except a rise to the Upper Ward. The earthwork of the Upper Ward was revetted in masonry in the late 12th or early 13th Century, and some of this can still be seen as a rough, low wall on the west side. A square gatehouse was also added, and in the mid- and late 13th Century a wall was built around the outer ward and the whole castle benefited by the addition of two round towers, a large and unusual bastion on the east corner, and, lastly, a massive double-towered gatehouse modelled on that at Caerphilly Castle, though inexpertly. The gatehouse entrance was walled up in the late 15th Century and a smaller entrance made in the wall alongside it; by then the castle had almost forgotten its military role, and the greatest threat was bands of brigands who could be deterred without an expensive and space-consuming gatehouse entrance.

Like many early Norman castles built near the sea or on a navigable river during the Anglo-Norman invasions of the 11th and 12th Centuries, Llanstephan Castle was to keep its importance long after the inland castles were completely taken over by the growing Welsh resistance. The Normans first arrived in present-day Carmarthenshire in 1093 but met very strong resistance, and it was not until 1106 that they were fully in control of Carmarthen, keeping that control until 1137. Welsh chronicles mention the name Llanstephan in a list of castles taken by Welsh chieftains from north Wales, but the castles in that list were all in Cardiganshire, and it is most likely that this was meant to be Castell Stephan, which was at Lampeter. There was certainly a Llanstephan Castle by 1146, for in that year it was captured by three princes of south Wales, Maredudd, Rhys, and Cadell, after they had successfully attacked Carmarthen Castle. The young warriors also had an opportunity to show their skill at defence when they held off an English attack on Llanstephan. Maredudd became quite a hero after it was recounted how he had thrown the English scaling-ladders down into the ditches below the walls—for the Welsh were not usually so successful at repelling attacks on strongholds in this way.

Llanstephan Castle's first known lord was Geoffrey Marmion, and it then passed to William de Camville of Devon who married Marmion's daughter Albreda near the end of the 12th Century. So began a few hundred years of complex and numerous changes of ownership. De Camville had Llanstephan snatched from him by the Lord Rhys of the South who broke with the English when Richard I became king in 1189. But Rhys was old and spent, and de Camville was back in his castle in

1189. He began to strengthen the defences and the earliest stonework at the castle probably dates from this time—the revetment of the upper ward. William de Camville gave the castle and town to his son Geoffrey, who had it captured from him by Llywelyn the Great during his whirlwind progress through Wales. But while Llywelyn remained very powerful in the north, the enmity and strength of the Marshall family, Earls of Pembroke, cut short his reign in the south, and the de Camvilles returned to Llanstephan Castle long before Llywelyn's death allowed so many other owners back into their northern castles.

The second William de Camville also suffered misfortune in the 1257 rising of Lord Rhys's descendants Maredudd ap Rhys and Maredudd ap Owain, when an English army sent to try to take the Welsh stronghold of Dynevor Castle was defeated in the battle of Coed Llathen. To the delight of the Welsh they found that they had killed two birds with one stone, for the English army had been largely made up of garrisons from their nearby castles, which were now left virtually defenceless. Llanstephan was soon taken, but Carmarthen held out, and eventually the Welsh could hold the region no longer and de Camville recovered his castle.

The remaining large-scale construction of Llanstephan's defences was carried out during the late 13th Century—the period of Edward I's conquest of Wales—by the second William de Camville and his son, the second Geoffrey, who played an important part in Edward's Welsh wars, although Llanstephan Castle itself was never directly involved. After the de Camville male line died out in 1338 Llanstephan Castle passed, by marriage and succession, to a Robert de Penres who came from an unimportant family which had nevertheless managed to acquire Penrice and Oxwich castles as well. These were all kept in such bad condition that Edward III thought they were a risk to the country's security (England was then at war with France), and ordered de Penres to repair them. He obviously did not get back into favour, however, for in 1377 he forfeited his lands after he was convicted, on what may have been a trumped-up charge, of the murder of a woman at Llanstephan. The Crown then gave Llanstephan Castle to the tutor of Richard II, but he was executed along with many of the king's advisers in 1388, and the second Robert de Penres paid a fine to get back his disgraced father's castle.

In the reign of Henry IV ownership of Llanstephan Castle became even more confused—it was apparently captured briefly by Owain Glyndwr's supporters, and tenancy was subsequently given to another Penres, Sir John, as a reward for retaking it from the rebels in 1403. He himself was soon captured by the Welsh; however, by 1408 Glyndwr's forces were finally ousted from the region and Sir John de Penres was back in Llanstephan. After he died the castle was claimed by Henry, Prince of Wales—though on what grounds was never certain, for claims to the castle were put by a few other people as well. The legal tangle must have been one of the worst in Wales, and only became resolved when Henry became Henry V and pressed his claim to possession justified by a string of reasons, including the unarguable one "or by any other cause". This certainly settled the matter, and Henry gave the castle to his brother, the Duke of Gloucester.

Llanstephan Castle remained Crown property for 200 years, though it was frequently granted for various lifetimes to nobles who had earned some reward or other. Some of the owners suffered misfortunes reminiscent of the earlier lords of the castle—the Duke of Suffolk was unseated and murdered in 1450, and after the Herberts, Earls of Pembroke, held it for twenty years, it was given in 1482 to the Prince of Wales who was soon after murdered with his brother in the Tower of London. The person responsible for blocking the the great gatehouse was probably Jasper Tewdwr, Duke of Bedford, who was granted the castle by his nephew Henry VII after his victory over Richard III at Bosworth.

After Owain Glyndwr, all Llanstephan Castle's battles seem to have been legal ones, and it deteriorated considerably. In 1860, for instance, farm buildings apparently stood all along the curtains. In 1959 the Government took over the care of the site from the owner, Major Fisher-Hock, and a large amount of restoration has been done.

**Llantrisant Castle,** *Llantrisant, Glamorgan. 8 miles north-west of Cardiff off A473.*

The last Welshman to have extensive control over this area was Hywel ap Meredith; he was deposed in about 1245 by Richard de Clare, who probably started Llantrisant Castle straight away, for the castle was mentioned in documents in 1246. It was attacked by rebels in 1315 and 1316, and was by then a masonry castle with a small inner bailey and a large outer bailey, the inner bailey being dominated by its large round keep. The site chosen, in a saddle between two hills, was a good defensive position, and a very picturesque one as well, as it overlooks the Vale of the Ely towards the Vale of Glamorgan. Edward II was caught near Llantrisant after he had left Chepstow Castle and the Despencers in his bid to escape from Queen Isabella and her followers, and was taken to Llantrisant Castle.

The main ruin now is a fragment of the round keep —perhaps the Raven Tower which the historian Leland mentioned as still being a prison during the Tudor period. (The castle is not far from the 1884 home of the famous eccentric Dr. Price, who is remembered for his efforts in many liberal causes including that to make cremation legal in Britain.)

**Llanvaches Castle,** *Llanvaches, Monmouthshire. 8 miles east-north-east of Newport off A48.*

With only traces of its foundations to be seen, and with no recorded history or description, Llanvaches is another "mystery" castle.

**Llawhaden Castle,** *Llawhaden, Pembrokeshire. 7½ miles east of Haverfordwest.*

The strange ruins of Llawhaden Castle have undergone a much needed restoration and now, in the distinct structures of four different periods, recollect a once-rich possession of the Bishops of St. David's. They also recollect the beginnings of Norman domination in that part of Wales, for the first ring motte was built to protect the estates after

one of Queen Matilda's chaplains, Bernard, began the spread of Norman influence when he was elected Bishop in 1115. Much of this early earthwork has since been levelled and built over; but its wooden stockade and buildings within the mound ring formed the Bishop's stronghold in 1175 when the Welsh churchman and historian Giraldus Cambrensis (Gerald de Barri) visited Llawhaden, then occupied by his uncle, Bishop David Fitzgerald.

The castle's first upheaval came in 1192 when it was captured by the Lord Rhys, Welsh ruler of the South; in those days the residences of churchmen were in no way immune, and certainly the Bishops of St. David's had a reputation as "fighting priests". (It is alleged that to comply with the prohibition against taking up the sword they used a "morning star", an unpleasant enough weapon made of a heavy spiked ball at the end of a chain.) Rhys destroyed the castle, but about two years later the Bishop had recovered Llawhaden. From excavations, it seems that early in the 13th Century, probably soon after the Bishop returned, a curtain was built where the wooden stockade had been, and this was flanked by semi-circular towers at regular intervals. The moat, however, survived, and is still there—a substantial earthwork 70 feet wide and about 25 feet deep.

After 1300 the castle and many other Bishops' residences underwent extravagant rebuilding which lasted many years and turned the modest stronghold into a lavish fortified mansion. The most peculiar aspect of these early 14th Century works is that they made no concession to the early castle's circular plan, or the circular shape of the earthworks. Consequently, since it was built as a series of rectangular blocks surrounding a courtyard, some of the towers project over the moat, while some are on the crest of the bank. The finished work provided the Bishop with comfortable apartments, rooms for guests, halls, a bakehouse, and quarters for a garrison—the castle had far more domestic buildings than was the norm for that period. Most of this is now quite badly ruined and detail work has long vanished; but it was probably built by David Martyn (who was Bishop from 1293 to 1328) since it is reportedly quite unlike works carried out either by Martyn's predecessor or his successor in other parts of the country.

*Llawhaden Castle, a stronghold of the Bishops of St. David's*

In the late 14th Century the only other major work was carried out—the extension of the gatehouse, whose shell can still be seen to its full height. Llawhaden Castle was listed as defensible in 1403 and was a Bishop's residence as late as 1503. According to tradition it was dismantled by Bishop Barlow in the mid-16th Century, after which the ruins were for some time used as a quarry, but were saved in the late 19th Century.

**Loughor Castle,** *Loughor, Glamorgan. 4 miles east-south-east of Llanelli off A484.*

The Normans took advantage of a natural mound looking very much like a motte, located at the nearest point to the sea where the Loughor river can be crossed, to build a small castle to watch over the crossing; quite likely, the Romans once occupied the same place. The earliest Norman castle was destroyed in 1151, and its successor was captured and ruined in 1215. The traces of a stone curtain and a projecting square tower probably date from the late 13th Century, and the castle was mentioned in a document of 1391, but after that date its history is unknown. The Department of the Environment has been restoring the remains.

**Madryn Castle,** *Garn, Caernarvonshire. 6 miles west of Pwllheli on Lleyn Peninsula.*

Madryn Castle, on the slope of Carn Fadryn (Madryn Mountain) is a Tudor mansion in an historic area. Nearby are the ruins of Castel Garn Fadryn, and on the summit of the mountain is a prehistoric fortress with a large stone called Arthur's Table—supposedly as important for Wales as the Stone of Scone is for Scotland, but its use was most probably religious and not political.

**Maescar Castle**—*see Cwm Camlais Castle.*

**Maesllwch Castle,** *Glasbury, Radnorshire. 4 miles west-south-west of Hay-on-Wye off A4153.*

A comparatively modern mansion (1829) in a very attractive setting.

**Manorbier Castle,** *Manorbier, Pembrokeshire. 5 miles east-south-east of Pembroke off B4585.*

Most of the extensive remains of Manorbier Castle date from the many additions made during the 13th Century, mainly by John de Barri. This stage of work apparently went on for some 50 years, fortunately not because of the interruptions of battle and siege, for much of it has withstood the ravages of time well. The first castle, of which a hall and a small tower beside the square gatehouse have remained, was founded at the beginning of the 12th Century, during the reign of Henry I, by the first Lord de Barri (who gave his name to the town now called Barry).

It is likely that it was built more as a baronial residence than a straightforward castle, and a historian once described it as a "most perfect model of an old Norman baron's residence, with all its appendages, church, mill, dove house, ponds, park and grove". Fine as it may have been, its principal claim to fame is that it was the birthplace, in about 1146, of Gerald de Barri, who became known (and has gone down in history) as Giraldus Cambrensis. Ecclesiastic, historian, topographer, intellectual, and passionately Welsh, Giraldus Cambrensis was widely respected, and his writings while recruiting for the Third Crusade with Archbishop Baldwin became the famous "Itinerary of Wales". Manorbier Castle as it now stands is considerably different from the one he knew, and which he described as ". . . excellently well defended by turrets and bulwarks . . . having on the northern and southern sides a fine fish-pond under its walls, as conspicuous for its grand appearance as for the depth of its waters . . ." and about which he concluded "that Manor Pirr is the pleasantest spot in Wales".

**Mathrafal Castle,** *Meifod, Montgomeryshire. 6 miles west-north-west of Welshpool at junction A495 and B4389.*

Mathrafal was once the seat of the princes of Powys, one of the three divisions of Wales, and the castle that occupied this site was both built and destroyed in 1212. It is set beside the River Banwy and was a low oval motte within a square earthwork. There are no traces of any masonry structure.

**Monmouth Castle,** *Monmouth, Monmouthsire. In town, on Castle Hill.*

Monmouth is probably the old Roman station of Blestium which guarded the crossing of Roman roads from Gloucester to Caerleon and from Caerwent to Wroxeter, but it was only after the Norman invasion that it achieved more lasting fame. The township and its first defences were established by

*East Tower and part of the curtain wall of Manorbier, castle of the Lords de Barri. Note the change in style of the masonry where a series of embrasures have been built up*

William FitzOsbern of Breteuil, Earl of Hereford and a powerful leader in the Conquest. The first castle was built during the period from 1067–71 when he overran so much of south-east Wales (see Chepstow Castle), and was one of a chain of fortifications holding his territory. That castle was probably a simple wooden structure on a motte, but no definite trace of either remains. Under the castle's protection Monmouth grew into a Norman settlement, a church was founded, and the town was listed in the Domesday Book of 1086 as part of Herefordshire, the castle then being held by William FitzBaderon for the Crown.

By 1100, however, Monmouth had almost completely broken away from Herefordshire and was the headquarters of the Marcher Lordship of Monmouth. FitzBaderon's descendants were to hold Monmouth Castle and surrounding estates until 1256, and between 1120 and 1150 they had built the Great Tower (or Norman Hall). In the first half of the 13th Century the first John of Monmouth built a large round tower, which had, according to the historian John Speed, "great height and strength". There is now no trace at all of this tower, but it was probably similar to the round towers which can be seen in the castles of Bronllys, Skenfrith, and Tretower. This was probably already part of the castle when it was captured by Richard Marshall, Earl of Pembroke, in 1233 during the struggles between supporters of the Crown and of the baronage—though the castle itself was apparently not involved in any attack, the issue of ownership being settled on a battlefield outside the town.

The last of the FitzBaderon family, the second John of Monmouth, had no male heir and granted the castle to Edward, son of Henry III, who was to become King Edward I, of dreadful memory in Wales. While it was in his possession it was captured by Simon de Montfort and his barons, Prince Edward regaining it not long after when he commanded the army which defeated Simon's forces at Kenilworth. Edward held the castle for

another two years until it was granted in 1267
(together with Grosmont, Skenfrith and White
Castles) to his younger brother Edmund 'Crouchback' when he was made Earl of Lancaster. Soon
after the Earl of Lancaster took over, the Great
Hall was added on the south side of the Great
Tower, and eighty years later, in 1350, the upper
part of the Tower was rebuilt.

Monmouth Castle had a royal birth within its walls
as notable as that within the walls of Caernarvon
Castle over 100 years previously, for in September
1387 the future King Henry V was born in the
Great Tower. Henry—victor at Agincourt, and
Shakespear's "Harry Monmouth"—was the son
of Henry of Bolingbroke, who had succeeded John
of Gaunt as Duke of Lancaster, and who was to
become Henry IV after forcing Richard II to abdicate in 1399 (see Conway Castle and Flint Castle).
Soon after Bolingbroke became King, the Welsh
under Owain Glyndwr rose throughout the
country; they were defeated near Grosmont, but in
1404 retaliated by massacring an English force at
Craig y Dorth, near Monmouth, and pursuing the
few survivors right up to Monmouth's town gates.
Under Henry VIII the Marcher Lordships were
abolished, but Monmouth remained an administrative centre and also had an assize court for hundreds
of years. In 1550, soon after his constitutional
reforms, Henry's surveyors found that most of
Monmouth Castle except the Great Hall (which
was regularly used as a court-room) was in very
bad condition. However, its defences were not put
to the test until the Civil War of 1642, when Monmouthshire declared itself loyal to Charles I, and
contributed very heavily to the Royalist cause.
Monmouth fell by a ruse to the Parliamentarians
in 1644—a disastrous loss for the Royalists, for
whom Monmouth was vital to their bid to hold
Southern Wales. The Parliamentarian garrison
under Colonel Massey fought many small battles
with the Royalists from nearby Raglan, but only
two months after Cromwell's forces had taken
Monmouth Colonel Massey was called away on
another campaign, and Lord Charles Somerset
retook Monmouth for the Royalists.

The town and castle remained in Royalist hands
for eleven months until October 1645 when they
surrendered to the Parliamentary governor of
Gloucester and an army of over 3,000 men. The
Parliamentarians had mined under part of the
castle, and prepared to blow it up, but discovered
huge quantities of arms, ammunition and provisions. The fall of Monmouth pointed to the end
for Charles I's supporters, although almost a year
was to pass before Raglan surrendered and all
South Wales and the Marches came under Parliamentary control. In the spring of 1647 an order
was given to slight the castle, and townspeople
joined the soldiers in pulling down the great Round
Tower, and demolishing various other parts. Nine
months later, it was recorded, at noon on a day
when most of the nearby inhabitants were at a
service, the west wall of the Great Tower collapsed,
perhaps weakened by the mining of two years
before.

After this destruction Monmouth Castle passed
into the possession of Henry Somerset, son of the
second Marquis of Worcester, an opportunist of
much ability who managed to befriend Cromwell
and also voted for the restoration of the monarchy
in 1660. It was he who built, on the site of the old
Round Tower, the imposing Great Castle House.
The Marquis was created Duke of Beaufort.
Eventually, by 1801, the House had become a girls'
school, and in 1875 the headquarters of the Royal
Monmouthshire Engineer Militia. Restoration of
the medieval ruins was begun by the Government
in 1913.

**Montgomery Castle,** *Montgomery, Montgomeryshire. 8 miles north-east of Newtown on B4385, in
town.*

The narrow ridge site of Montgomery Castle was a
sought-after defensive position from the earliest
days of the Norman conquest, although the first
castle, a motte and bailey structure begun by
Roger de Montmorency in 1072, was at the foot of
Castle Hill where its earthwork remains can still be
seen. This castle and the first Norman settlement
were soon taken by the Welsh, but almost as

quickly retaken by the Normans led by Baldwyn de Boller, who greatly increased the fortifications. His tenure gave the castle its alternative name of Baldwyn's Castle, or "Balwy", and Welshmen often call the town Trefaldwyn (Baldwin's Town). Twenty years later it was again attacked by the Welsh in another borderland battle, but they were once more beaten back by William II (Rufus) and his army. Border battles kept raging across the area, with the Welsh gradually giving way, and each successor to the castle repairing the damage he had caused in capturing it.

The ruins that can now be seen date from later than these Norman battles, and were all erected around 1225, during the reign of Henry III. There are now only fragments of a tower and some portions of walls left; but it once boasted five wards in line on the ridge, possibly all walled, and the third and fourth wards certainly were—with a strong outer wall defended by three solid round towers, enclosing a small inner ward with a great round tower. This castle was attacked and badly burnt and damaged by the Welsh under Llywelyn the Great in 1228, but after that it stayed in English hands. It eventually became one of the possessions of the Mortimers, and was subsequently the home of the Herberts. One of these, Lord Herbert of Cherbury, garrisoned Montgomery Castle for Charles I in the Civil War; but he was clearly a man with a delicate understanding of the fortunes of his times, and surrendered the castle as soon as Sir Thomas Myddelton demanded it. Other Royalists were not so acquiescent, and besieged the castle their subtle comrade had so recently vacated; but a relief force of Parliamentarians drove them off leaving some 500 dead. In 1649, by Parliamentary order, Montgomery Castle was destroyed.

**Morlais Castle,** *Merthyr Tydfil, Glamorgan. 2 miles north of Merthyr Tydfil.*

Overlooking the Taf gorge and gazing towards the

*Narberth Castle*

Brecon Beacons are the ruins of a once powerful Edwardian baronial castle. It was begun by Gilbert de Clare, and though it was probably never finished the castle's great round keep was surrounded by four round towers, substantial earthworks and an outer bailey. Today only part of the curtain around the inner bailey survives, along with two of its round towers. De Clare was one of the great Marcher barons who held down Wales after Edward's conquest, and the castle was probably started in about 1287. The only documented history of the castle is the role it played in the long and frequently violent legal dispute between de Clare and the Earl of Hereford, de Bohun. This dispute so angered Edward I (who often had to remind the Barons that they were, after all, still his subjects) that he undertook a forced march from North Wales to Morlais, fined both Earls heavily, and made them forfeit much of their land. The remains of the old well shaft can still be seen in the inner bailey, and one of the towers has a room with a vaulted roof supported by a central pillar.

**Narberth Castle,** *Narberth, Pembrokeshire. In town 8½ miles north of Tenby off A478.*

Narberth Castle, now largely ruined, was built in the mid- or late 13th Century, perhaps by Sir Andrew Perrot, with a single ward, a round keep and four or five round towers. Narberth was once held by Roger Mortimer, favourite of Queen Isabella, who plotted with her the downfall of her husband King Edward II.

**Neath Castle,** *Neath, Glamorgan. In town, 6 miles north-east of Swansea.*

The founder of Neath Abbey, Richard de Granville, also founded the first castle here in 1129, but the remains of a gateway and its flanking towers date from the early 13th Century. The castle seems to have taken no part in the two major campaigns of Edward I, but was captured by the Welsh in local risings in 1231 and 1321, and was unsuccessfully attacked in 1258. It was listed in the review of defences in 1404 as "tenable".

**Nevern Castle**—*see Castell Nanhyfer.*

**Newcastle Emlyn Castle,** *Newcastle Emlyn, Carmarthenshire. 9 miles east-south-east of Cardigan on A475.*

The district of Emlyn had come under the control of the powerful Marshalls, Earls of Pembroke (see Cilgerran Castle and Chepstow Castle) in 1223, and from them it was granted to grandsons of the Lord Rhys. The second grandson, Maredudd ap Rhys of Dynevor, built the "new" castle in 1240, upstream from Cilgerran, within an S-bend of the Teifi that almost made a complete natural moat. Maredudd's son Rhys ap Maredudd tried to lead an uprising after Edward I's conquest of 1282, and Newcastle Emlyn Castle was captured by the English in 1287. They did not easily win the castle, for it changed hands three times in the year, finally succumbing to the battering of a siege engine which had been dragged to the walls from Dryslwyn Castle.

The castle up to that stage had been a simple quadrilateral ward with an outer enclosure, but at the beginning of the 14th Century, and again from

1347–49, the English enlarged the defences with a double-towered gatehouse and a small polygonal tower. In 1403 the Welsh once again took the castle, during Owain Glyndwr's revolt, and it was badly damaged during the struggle. For many years it was neglected, but Henry VII gave it to Sir Rhys ap Thomas in 1485 and he rebuilt it, thereafter using it as one of his favourite residences. The castle next saw battle in the Civil War, held out until the Parliamentarians captured it in 1644, and was one of the hundreds they subsequently slighted. Now the ruins are covered in ivy and offer impressive views.

**Newcastle,** *Bridgend, Glamorgan, north end of town off A4063.*

The origins of the ruined castle and its name are confused and obscure. The first mention seems to be in 1106, in a confirmation of grants to the conqueror of Glamorgan, Robert FitzHamon. This document from Henry I's court mentions "Church of Newcastle" (Ecclesiam de Novo Castello), so some castle existed then. The present ruins, however, are dated to the second half of the 12th Century, through evidence provided by its structure, and they must therefore be the ruins of a castle still newer than the 1106 Newcastle. But it is not at all clear whether, prior to 1106, the site had a still older castle on it which was replaced, giving it the name Newcastle, or whether another castle already existed nearby, and when one was built about 1106 it was called Newcastle to distinguish it. This last is the most likely, and it is possible that the older castle was on the site on which Payn de Turbeville founded Coity Castle, for Coity can easily be seen from Newcastle.

Together with Coity and Ogmore Castles (and the fortified Priory at Ewenny), Newcastle defended the line of the Ogmore and the Ewenny which for some time must have marked the western boundary of the Norman conquest. Newcastle overlooks the most suitable ford, and it must have been an important stronghold, for many of the old roads and tracks converged on this crossing. But even the site of the 1106 castle is unknown; work on the present ruins disclosed no earthworks or postholes

which should have been left by an earlier castle (which, in 1106, would most likely not have had any stone work). The present ruins probably date from after 1154, it being unlikely that they would have been started during Stephen's reign, and their design reflecting more the time of Henry II.

Perhaps the thick polygonal curtain which forms the castle at Bridgend lies directly on the earlier earthworks; but whatever the original form, the present ruins are rather bare. The east wall is long and straight, along the top of a steep slope, and turns at right angles at its southern end towards the gateway 50 feet away. The rest of the curtain makes, by nine short straight sections, a long curve back to the north end of the straight east wall. Two of the nine sections are large, almost square towers. The gateway in the south-east is a feature of the ruins, for it is one of the few surviving gateways which were decorated in the elaborate style of that 12th Century period, and must have been completed in about 1175. The tower nearest the gateway was probably the keep, though it is the same size as the other tower on the curtain. Originally both towers were only entered at the first storey level, though the keep had a ground floor entrance put in at a later date.

The courtyard must have contained other buildings needed by the garrison, but only a small part of a fairly large room, against the east wall, survives from this period, and this was probably the hall. South of this are the remains of some of the extensive modifications made in the 16th Century.

**Newport Castle,** *Newport, Monmouthshire. On river bank at east end of High Street.*

The Norman invaders of Glamorgan founded Newport Castle in 1172; its original form is uncertain, since it was rebuilt during the 14th and 15th Centuries, particularly during the Wars of the Roses. It must have been a square stone castle, but now only one face of it remains, with a tower containing the water gate and the chapel above it, and another, the Bridge Tower, showing excellent decorated 15th Century windows. Newport Castle weathered a number of attacks and captures during the 13th Century, again in 1321, and once more, by Owain Glyndwr, in 1404. Against the remaining wall is a small public garden with seats.

**Newport Castle,** *Newport, Pembrokeshire. 6 miles east of Fishguard off A487.*

The successor to Nevern Castle is now identified by the remains of three round towers—one of which was very large—and a twin-towered gatehouse. It was founded by William de Turribus in the early 13th Century, but the gatehouse was an addition of the latter part of the century. The ruins were built into a mansion in 1859.

**New Radnor Castle,** *New Radnor, Radnorshire. 9½ miles east of Llandrindod Wells on A44.*

By present standards there is nothing "new" about the town of New Radnor, for it was possibly founded before the Norman invasion; some sources

*Newcastle Emlyn, built in 1240 in a bend of the river Teifi. It saw hard fighting in 1287, changing hands three times in that year*

111

attribute it to Harald, Earl of Hereford, after he had destroyed what then became Old Radnor. Other sources say that its similarity to Winchelsea in Sussex means that its founder was undoubtedly one of the de Braose family—one of the most hated Norman broods—who seized the area in about 1200. This is the more likely date, for although New Radnor was first mentioned as a town in 1291, there is a mention of a plain Radnor being rebuilt in 1233, and perhaps the site was changed then. The castle was doubtless built simultaneously but offers no clues, since except for the remains of the earthworks there is nothing left of it. But it was apparently a powerful masonry castle, and even if its history is obscured by the one at Old Radnor, Castle Nimble, it does seem that this castle was captured by the Welsh in 1264 and again in 1322. It was mentioned as defensible in 1402 and 1405, but was greatly damaged by Owain Glyndwr after the battle of Pilleth. New Radnor was a Royalist stronghold in the Civil War, and was wrecked by Cromwell's artillery before it surrendered to the Parliamentarians.

*Founded by William de Turribus in the early 13th Century, Newport Castle survives as three ruined towers and this gatehouse*

**Ogmore Castle,** *Ogmore, Glamorgan. 2 miles south-south-west of Bridgend on B4524.*

Ogmore Castle was situated in a strangely remote part of its original lordship, but its positioning was strategically important, for it formed the defence of the western boundary of Glamorgan together with Newcastle at Bridgend, Coity Castle, and the fortified monastery of Ewenny. These strongholds guarded routes and fords across the Ewenny and Ogmore rivers, Ogmore Castle guarding the stepping stones across the Ewenny as well as the ford across the Ogmore at nearby Merthyr Mawr.

The castle is now particularly known for its keep— one of the earliest 12th Century stone keeps in Wales—a rectangular tower three stories high, made with large irregular boulders set in mortar. One of the walls still stands to a height of about 40 feet, though the others have partly collapsed. The interior of the ground floor, as became the normal defensive pattern, could originally only be reached through a trapdoor from the first floor. The tower had its roof raised and a third storey put in at some early stage, for the line of the original gutter can still be seen.

In another 12th Century building in the inner ward an inscribed pre-Norman cross base was found, having been used as the floor of a furnace. The original stone is now in the National Museum of Wales, but a replica was cast and placed next to the kiln. In the early 13th Century domestic buildings were added to the inner ward and it was surrounded by a rather weak curtain, though the earthwork defences, including the moat on three sides and the Ewenny River on the north side, probably made this sufficient. The moated outer ward had a lime kiln added in the late 13th Century, and a courthouse was built early in the 15th Century.

Ogmore's first castle was built in about 1116 by William de Londres, and this was probably at first only earthworks and ditches, though the keep must have come soon afterwards. William's son, Maurice, still in the reign of Henry I, gained Kidwelly and the castle built there by Roger, Bishop of Salisbury. From then on the fortunes of Ogmore were tied up with Kidwelly, the de Londres family, with Walter de Braose, the tragic Hawise, the Chaworths, until it became part of the Honour of Lancaster (see Kidwelly Castle). It had little later history of note, being used mainly as a prison, and for its courthouse. The castle and the stepping stones were placed in the care of the Government by the Duchy of Lancaster in 1928.

**Old Beaupre Castle**—*see Beaupre Castle.*

**Old Castle,** *Llanblethian, Glamorgan. ½ mile south-east of Cowbridge.*

Some historians in Tudor times mentioned a castle here, Leland calling it Llygod Castle, and it is also shown in the background of a popular 18th Century painting. It was presumably the predecessor of Llanblethian Castle, and part of it might perhaps be a portion of the remains of an ancient fort. No details are known of either the exact site or its history.

**Old Radnor Castle**—*see Castle Nimble.*

**Oxwich Castle,** *Oxwich, Glamorgan. 11 miles south-west of Swansea.*

The early castle at Oxwich belonged to a relatively minor family of landowners, whose estates were split up when one of them, Richard de Penres, took Penrice Castle for himself on his marriage to the heiress to Llanstephan Castle, while Oxwich

*Ogmore Castle, with one of the earliest 12th Century stone keeps in Wales, guarded the crossings of the rivers Ewenny and Ogmore*

Castle was left for the rest of his family. It was presumably a sacrifice they all made to become associated with the far more noble de Camvilles—but a sacrifice in vain, for Richard's son neglected his estate, incurred the displeasure of Edward III, and lost his estates on being found guilty of murder —although there was some doubt over the verdict, which saved his life.

Oxwich became associated with Penrice again in the 16th Century when in 1541 the holders of Penrice built a large manor house among the remnants of Oxwich Castle; but part of the curtain, the gatehouse and a fragment of the great tower in the Tudor house remain.

**Oystermouth Castle,** *Mumbles, Glamorgan. 4 miles south-west of Swansea off A4067.*

The Normans soon dominated southern Wales, and the first castle was probably set up on this commanding, rocky site before the end of the 11th Century, perhaps by Henry Beaumont. Whatever existed there before, it was destroyed by the Welsh in 1287 during that year's brief but violent rising. The present substantial ruins date from the reconstruction after that date, and are unusual in that the gatehouse and a large rectangular tower enclose a masonry ward by being linked by a very high wall,

undefended by towers. (The gatehouse did once have two round towers which were, for some reason, demolished during one of the many periods of alteration which went on well into the 16th Century, and which included the raising of the wall in the 14th Century.) The large, rectangular, three-storied tower contained the hall, main apartments, and the chapel in which can still be seen a traceried window and the stone basin used in the rinsing of the chalice during services.

# P

**Painscastle,** *Painscastle, Radnorshire. 4½ miles north-west of Hay-on-Wye.*

This was a strong motte and bailey castle, and the few traces of masonry left suggest that the motte once bore a round keep, and that there was at least one further tower. Although it was not mentioned in documents before 1191, it could have been built before 1137 by Payn FitzJohn; and some suggest its builder was Matilda de Breos, for two alternate names are Maud's Castle, and Castrum Matildis. At the end of the 12th Century Painscastle was held by the hated Marcher Lord, William de Braose, and was besieged by Gwenwynwyn of Powys (central Wales), whose cousin Trahaiarn had been dragged through Brecon tied to the tail of a horse, and then beheaded, all at the order of de Braose. But Gwenwynwyn was unable to exact his revenge. Painscastle held, and the Normans stirred up the princes of the south against the men of Powys. At Painscastle the grim alliance of the men of Deheubarth (the South) and the Normans massacred the men of Powys.
Painscastle was eventually captured in 1215, and then rebuilt in 1231 as a stronger stone castle.

Another rising in 1265 caused much destruction, but in 1403 it was listed as defensible.

**Pembroke Castle,** *Pembroke, Pembrokeshire. On western edge of town near junction of A4139 and B4320.*

Pembroke Castle is on a well-chosen site that is almost a fortress itself, a mass of rock with precipitous sides plunging down to the tidal waters of the Pembroke River and Milford Haven. This site, with the formidable defences of the castle itself, made Pembroke almost impregnable, and one of the largest and strongest fortresses in Wales. The irregular shape of the outer curtain followed the shape of the rock, and it was protected by five large round towers and a gatehouse. The gatehouse and curtain between the outer and inner baileys have now almost disappeared. The south side of the outer curtain—the inland end away from the apex of the rock, and therefore the most vulnerable—was double-walled, an extra eight feet added to the inside giving it a total thickness of fifteen feet.

The most outstanding feature of the imposing ruins is the enormous round keep in the triangular inner bailey at the north end of the site. This part of the defences was built near the end of the 12th Century; the outer bailey with its towers, remarkable gatehouse, and a strange rectangular projection with two round turrets on the east curtain, was built in the mid-13th Century. The keep is regarded as the finest medieval round tower in the British Isles. Four stories high, it still towers 80 feet above its widely spread plinth. The wall is 20 feet thick at the base, which has a diameter of 53 feet, and even

*Oxwich Castle was owned in medieval times by the de Penres family, ambitious men whose determined social climbing led indirectly to a trumped-up murder charge*

at the first storey it is over 14 feet thick. A spiral staircase in the thickness of the wall provides access to the floors and the roof, and to the basement which is slightly below ground level. Entrance to the keep was by drawbridge to the first floor, which was only lit by two arrowholes. East of the keep are two adjacent halls (they share a wall), and underneath the outer hall, whose one wall forms a part of the curtain, is a large cavern, called Wogan, which has been cut out of the rock. A winding stair led to it from the hall, and originally there was doubtless a gate to the river through which provisions could be taken in or secret escape made. From the inner hall, a wing led to a door in the keep at the level of its third storey.

The massive fortifications of Pembroke Castle are still very evident, and they are a far cry from the first castle erected there in 1097 by Arnulph de

Montgomery, which was described as "a slender fortress with stakes and turf". Its early history is obscure and uneventful—largely because it was too powerful to get involved in minor skirmishes. Henry II used it as a base before sailing from it to Ireland in 1172, and King John visited the castle as well. Pembroke was closely involved, however, in the dawning of the Tudor age. In the Wars of the Roses the Lancastrians suffered a number of crushing defeats, the worst of which was the battle of Tewkesbury in 1471, when Henry, the former King Henry VI, was captured and subsequently stabbed to death in the Tower. That left Henry Tudor, Earl of Richmond, sole Lancastrian claimant to the throne, and he and his uncle Jasper Tudor (Tewdwr) fled to Pembroke Castle where Henry had been born. The Yorkists besieged the castle, but Henry and Jasper were rescued and escaped to France.

At that time the most powerful figure in South Wales was Rhys ap Thomas, Lord of the South, and in 1483 he swore allegiance to Richard III, vowing that Henry would only return to Wales "over his body". In 1485 Henry Tudor did return to Wales with Jasper to reclaim the Lancastrian crown. He landed at Milford Haven with 2,000 men and Pembrokeshire welcomed him with open arms, seeing at last the chance to have a Welshman on the throne of England and Wales. The Bishop of St. David's was as enthusiastic as the rest, and absolved Rhys ap Thomas from his oath to Richard, since Richard was "a usurper and a murderer" (of the Princes in the Tower of London). Rhys made doubly certain of that by lying on the ground at Pembroke, and inviting Henry to step over his body. After that Sir Rhys was one of Henry's most powerful allies, and the two of them made a two-pronged march northwards, joining up at Shrewsbury with a gathered army of 5,000. From there they went to Bosworth where, on 22nd August, Henry defeated Richard and his far larger army. Richard was killed, Henry became Henry VII, the Tudor age began, and an era of peace came to Wales.

The next time that Pembroke found itself so involved in the affairs of the nation was the Civil War of 1642. Pembroke was one of the few castles in Wales not held for the Royalists, the Mayor of Pembroke, Poyer, garrisoning it for the Parlia-mentarians. Nevertheless, when the second stage of the war between Charles I and Cromwell's Parliamentary forces broke out in 1648, Poyer changed his allegiance and held Pembroke for the Royalists. This was a bad blow to Cromwell, and since Pembroke was considered to be almost impregnable, it took all his force and expertise to achieve its downfall. Even then the siege went on for six weeks and only succeeded when the food supply was cut off, and when a traitor directed artillery fire to block the staircase leading from the hall to the Wogan cavern, which held the castle's water supply. After capturing the town and the castle, Cromwell slighted it (and also wrecked Haverfordwest Castle, to prevent the same thing happening there). Poyer and two of his turncoat accomplices were sent to Windsor and condemned to death, but the Army Council decided to execute only one of them. Lots were drawn with one blank piece of paper and two with the words "Life given by God". The blank piece was drawn by Poyer, and he was shot in Covent Garden a few days later.

**Pen y Castell,** *Llanilar, Cardiganshire. 5½ miles south-east of Aberystwyth off A485.*

These are the remains of a small fort divided by an open-cast cut. It may be the castle of Garth Grugyn which was built in 1242, though some experts point out that it was too far from the township of Crugyn (now Craigwen) for it to be that 13th Century (according to documents) castle.

**Penard Castle,** *Parkmill, Glamorgan. 8 miles west-south-west of Swansea.*

Penard Castle is the rather uninteresting ruin of an insignificant castle which seems to have had no history of consequence. It was a weakly built castle which probably developed from a hall within a ring earthwork, and in the 13th Century developed a twin-towered gatehouse and a small round turret.

It was ruined in the 16th Century.

**Pencelli Castle,** *Pencelli, Breconshire. 4 miles south-east of Brecon on B4558.*

The remains of Pencelli Castle have been built into farm buildings; it was a motte and bailey castle with a masonry tower on the motte, and the walled bailey seems to have had an impressive double-towered gatehouse. It was captured by the Welsh during minor risings in 1215, 1233 and 1322.

**Pencoed Castle,** *Llanmartin, Monmouthshire. 6½ miles east of Newport off B4245.*

The origins and history of Pencoed Castle are not known, but it must have been a small castle. One of its 13th Century towers and a part of its curtain were incorporated in a large unfortified 16th Century house.

**Penhow Castle,** *Penhow, Monmouthshire. 7½ miles east of Newport on A48.*

Penhow Castle was a small fortification whose ward and oblong tower were built in the 13th Century, with other additions being made in and after the 15th Century. The tower, or keep, is now badly ruined, but the castle seems to have no recorded history.

**Penlle'r Castell,** *Cwmgors, Glamorgan. 10 miles north of Swansea.*

This was probably a late 13th Century stronghold garrisoned by a Marcher Lord against one of his rivals, and is unlikely even to have been a permanent fortification. It perhaps had two square towers, but these were probably made of dry stone walls, as there is no evidence of mortaring. The flat platform forming the castle base was defended by deep ditches, and there are impressive views from the summit (the name means "summit of the place of the castle").

**Penllyn Castle,** *Penllyn, Glamorgan. 5 miles east-south-east of Bridgend.*

One remaining corner of a very early rectangular tower—perhaps early 12th Century, and crudely built—has been incorporated into a later residential building. There is apparently no recorded history of the old fortification, and it is impossible to trace its original character.

**Penmarc Castle,** *Penmarc, Glamorgan. 4 miles west-north-west of Barry.*

The few remains here are from a castle whose earthworks must once have covered a large area, but only part of the stone wall now survives, and there are traces of a round tower. The castle belonged to a knight of Glamorgan, de Umfraville, whose family strongly opposed King John.

**Penrhyn Castle,** *Bangor, Caernarvonshire. 1 mile east of Bangor off A55.*

Although Penrhyn Castle is actually a massive early Victorian mansion, the site is reputed to have ancient associations—a Welsh prince of A.D. 720 is said to have had his palace here, and a nearby 17th Century residence incorporates a medieval house that traditionally belonged to Llywelyn the Great. According to tradition, it was a steward of Llywelyn's who started the family of Penrhyn; one of them, Ednyfed Fychan, had a descendant called Gwilym ap Gruffydd who is regarded as the true founder. In the 17th Century John Williams (who became Archbishop of York—see Conway Castle) bought the estate, and eventually a Richard Pennant married a descendant of the Archbishop. He started up the slate quarries which brought fame and prosperity. Richard Pennant's great nephew

George Hay Dawkins Pennant inherited the estate, and viewed with displeasure the 17th Century Gothic Revival residence which had used Llywelyn's medieval house.

Dawkins Pennant commissioned Thomas Hopper to design a new mansion, and the gigantic, extravagant building that is now Penrhyn Castle resulted. Hopper spared neither his imagination nor his client's money, for the interiors are vast, opulent, theatrical and often staggering. Nor did Hopper stop at the structure itself, for he designed all the interior decoration and commissioned the furniture as well. The "castle" used local materials as much as possible: oak from the estates' forests, Mona marble from Anglesey, and slate from the family's quarries—tribute to this product even extending to a bedstead carved out of solid slate, and weighing all of four tons! The story is recounted that Queen Victoria was offered the bed, but refused it with the comment "It is interesting but uninviting".

Apart from the mixture of Victorian supersaturation and the imitation of Norman exteriors mixed with numerous other periods, Penrhyn Castle has a huge and unique collection of dolls

*The massive fortifications of Pembroke Castle, where Jasper Tewdwr and his nephew—later Henry VII—were besieged by the Yorkists after Tewkesbury*

from all over the world, a museum of old steam engines, and 40 acres of park and gardens. The estate is administered by the National Trust, having been given to the Trust by the Treasury, to whom it had been granted in lieu of death duties in 1951, and forms part of the Ysbyty Estates, at 41,727 acres the largest single property owned by the National Trust.

**Penrice Castle,** *Penrice, Glamorgan. 11 miles west-south-west of Swansea off A4118.*

Penrice Castle was the ancestral home of the de Penres family, whose main claims to historical fame are described elsewhere (see Llanstephan Castle). After marrying into the powerful de Camville family, Robert de Penres incurred the wrath of Edward III in 1367 by allowing his castles to fall into such disrepair that the safety of the realm was said to be endangered. Penrice was confiscated, along with Robert's other estates, in 1377, when he was convicted under dubious circumstances of the murder of a woman at Llanstephan seven years previously.

The "murderer's" son, another Robert de Penres, bought back the estates in 1391, but soon afterwards they reverted to the Crown as Robert had no heirs. When Richard de Penres had married Eleanor de Camville, he had kept Penrice Castle. Eventually the whole family seems to have flowed back together again. One of the Oxwich de Penres became established at Llanstephan in 1400, and in 1541 the holders of Penrice built a large manor house in the ruins of Oxwich Castle.

Penrice itself was on a foreland site, and was built as the successor to the earthwork fortification of nearby Mounty Brough. The ruins of the round keep of the mid-13th Century and the double-towered gatehouse, two round towers and five small round turrets of fifty years later were joined by a much more modern building.

**Pentrefoelas Castle,** *Pentrefoelas, Denbighshire. 5½ miles south-east of Betwys-y-Coed off B5113.*

Pentrefoelas Castle has no recorded history, though it is thought likely that it was already abandoned by 1198. It had a large motte with a ring wall, but the bailey was small.

**Picton Castle,** *Haverfordwest, Pembrokeshire. 3½ miles east-south-east of Haverfordwest.*

The first castle on this site has long since vanished, but it was established in the reign of William II ("Rufus") by William de Picton. De Picton was a Norman knight who accompanied Arnulph de Montgomery into south-west Wales. De Montgomery founded the first Pembroke Castle in 1097, while de Picton moved further north. It is likely that Picton Castle was a Welsh stronghold, and that de Picton moved in, and stayed in, after he had ousted the castle's original owners.

The substantial ruins of the large, solid castle-block, with its four attached round towers and the small double-towered gatehouse, date from the late 13th Century or even early 14th Century. The history of the earlier castle is unknown, but Picton Castle did succeed the nearby Wiston Castle, and the last mention of that castle was in 1220 when it was recorded that it was to be rebuilt. It never was, and perhaps the move took place soon after, with work on the new Picton Castle beginning after Edward I's victories of 1282–83. The castle changed hands during Owain Glyndwr's revolt in 1403, but it was not until the Civil War between Charles I and his Parliament that Picton Castle became truly embroiled in national events. Sir Richard Philipps garrisoned the castle for the Royalists, and after it had changed hands in the early stages, the Parliamentarians besieged it. The siege was long, and the Royalists seemed to be holding out until they were beaten by the capture of a hostage. The castle nursery occupied one of the lower rooms and had a window looking away from the walls. A Parliamentary messenger, carrying a flag of truce, rode up to the window one day when the nursemaid held the infant Erasmus Philipps in her arms. To receive the message she opened the window and leant out, stretching towards the horseman. Suddenly he snatched the child and galloped back to his camp. The demand to surrender or sacrifice the child soon arrived, and the castle immediately surrendered. The Parliamentarians were apparently moved by the garrison's stand, and by the unhesitating way they gave themselves up to save the child—and, no doubt, were troubled by their own tactics—so they allowed the garrison the full honours of war, and even arranged that Picton Castle, unlike most, should not be slighted.

**Pipton Castle,** *Aberllynfi, Breconshire. 9½ miles north-east of Brecon off A4079.*

These ruins may not even be of a castle, for they show only the remains of a stone structure which may or may not have been a tower. It is possible that this is the same site as the Periton Castle mentioned in documents in 1233, though not subsequently.

**Pointz Castle,** *Pen-y-cwm, Pembrokeshire. 9 miles north-west of Haverfordwest off A487.*

Also called Punch Castle, these fragmentary ruins have no recorded history, and offer no hints as to their structure or origin.

**Porthamal Castle,** *Talgarth, Breconshire. 8 miles north-east of Brecon off A4078.*

Probably this was not a castle but a "stronghouse", deriving its slight defensive strength from its walled enclosure which was topped with battlements. The gateway and part of the curtain remain, and it was most likely built in the 15th Century.

**Porth Tre-castell,** *Aberffraw, Anglesey. 10 miles south-east of Holyhead off A4080.*

Porth Tre-castell is not a castle, nor even a fortified house, but one of the many sandy-floored, rock-bound coves on this stretch of the coast. There is no trace of a castle in the vicinity.

**Powis Castle,** *Welshpool, Montgomeryshire. On south edge of town.*

Powis Castle has come a long way from its beginnings as a motte and bailey stronghold not far short of 800 years ago; it shows much evidence of the long centuries of changing techniques and priorities, of additions and alterations, and of 500 unbroken years of habitation.

Its beginnings, however, are uncertain. Two mottes nearby (one known as Welshpool or Domen Castell, a mile away, the other in the grounds of the park) are involved in the early stages; some succession between the three took place, and a castle of Trallwng (the old name for Welshpool) was documented in 1196. Perhaps it goes back to a castle begun by Cadrogan in 1109, and completed only after his death. This was captured in 1191 after a long siege by English forces, but retaken in 1196 by Welshmen of Powisland. These Welsh became collaborators of the English, according to one source, and it was only in 1275 that the hold was again in loyal Welsh possession, when it was captured and destroyed by Llywelyn Prince of Wales.

After Edward I's success over the Welsh two years later the castle reverted to Gruffydd ap Gwenwynwyn, of the Powis family that had allied with the English. For the remainder of the 13th Century Gruffydd and his son Owain enlarged and changed the castle considerably, setting the frame on which all the future generations built. The medieval castle then comprised two wards, a double-towered gatehouse leading into the small, rounded inner ward and a round tower. It also acquired at this time one of its alternative names—Castell Coch, for the red sandstone of which it was made.

Powis Castle seems to have been a peaceful place, for little of military importance happened in the area despite its proximity to the border. One of the most significant events in its history was when it was acquired by the famous Herbert family. Sir Edward Herbert, a son of the Earl of Pembroke, bought Powis Castle in 1587. He began many alterations to bring the castle up to the standard of luxury expected in those Elizabethan years. The fine, panelled Long Gallery was built at this stage. Sir Edward's son William Herbert was created Baron Powis in 1629, and he fortified and garrisoned the castle for the Royalists when the Civil War broke out in 1642. The castle was attacked in 1644; the western gateway was completely destroyed, and the garrison surrendered to the Parliamentarian commander, Sir Thomas Myddelton. Cromwell fortunately spared Powis Castle the fate of slighting.

A new stage of building began with the next William Herbert, the third Baron Powis, in 1667, with the reconstruction of the western terrace and the construction of the State Bedroom, the Grand Staircase, and the east portal. The return of Charles II from Saint-Germain in France influenced landscaping to reflect the techniques he had so admired during his exile, and Lord Powis ordered William Winde to plan the terracing on the castle's southern side (Winde was also responsible for some of the internal additions). William became Earl of Powis in 1674, and Marquess in 1687. He was sent to the Tower of London for suspected complicity in the Popish Plot. In 1688 he escaped Britain and fled to France out of loyalty to James II. Lady Powis, a Lady of the Bedchamber, was given charge of the Prince of Wales, and managed to smuggle him to Versailles. The estates then temporarily passed out of the hands of the Herberts in 1696 when they were conferred by William III on his nephew, the Earl of Rochford.

It used to be thought that it was the Rochfords who so transformed Powis Castle between 1696 and 1722, but few of the heads of the family stayed there for long, though the Lanscroon murals were doubtless commissioned by them. When George I came to the throne in 1714 he reinstated William, son of the first Marquess of Powis, at which the Rochfords ransacked the castle of all its valuable documents and furniture. William, the second Marquess of Powis, carried on his father's work on the castle, and finished the Blue Room and the terraces and hanging gardens. "Capability" Brown was reputed to have carried out much of the external renovation and landscaping, though there is also considerable evidence that this could all have

*Powis Castle, where five centuries of occupation and alterations have changed a 13th Century Welsh stronghold into an elegant showplace noted for its fine interiors*

been the work of Winde, under the first Marquess at the end of the 17th Century.

In 1801 the Powis estates passed to Henrietta Antonia, daughter of the distinguished politician Henry Arthur Herbert, a descendant of Baron Herbert of Cherbury, the Royalist who had garrisoned Montgomery Castle in the Civil War. She married Edward, the son of Clive of India, and many relics and possessions of Lord Clive's came to Powis Castle. Edward Clive was created Earl of Powis in 1802 and the family name of Clive disappeared in 1807 when his son adopted the name of Herbert. In 1891 the son of Lieutenant-General Sir Percy Herbert became the 4th Earl of Powis, and the most extensive modifications for two hundred years were undertaken for him by G. F. Bodley. The interior was remodelled, together with the creation of the Dining Room and the Oak Drawing Room, and the enlarging of the East Tower.

Powis Castle was given to the National Trust by the 4th Earl in 1952, the year of his death. The principal contents of the castle were transferred to the Trust by the Treasury in 1965, and the 5th Earl, great-great-great grandson of Lord Clive, lives at Powis Castle. With its red sandstone, the evidence of five centuries of occupation, its striking and sumptuous interiors, the superb formal gardens, and the relics of Clive of India, Powis Castle offers a wealth of features.

**Prestatyn Castle,** *Prestatyn, Flintshire. 4 miles east of Rhyl on A548.*

The low motte inside a rectangular bailey was not built on a very good site; it was marshy, and the

whole castle provided only a weak defence. It inevitably had a short career. The castle is attributed to Robert Banastre in 1164; it was destroyed in 1167 and was probably never used beyond the end of the 12th Century. For all the shortness of its history, it recalls one of the saddest lost hopes of Welsh history. It was held soon after it was built by a prince of Powys, Owain Cyfeiliog (who was described by Giraldus Cambrensis in 1188 as one of the wisest and best of the princes of Wales). The rulers of Powys, the central part of Wales and the ancient kingdom, always tried to unite Gwynedd (the north) and Deheubarth (the south) into one state. But when Welsh forces gained notable victories against Henry II and achieved a position of considerable bargaining power, the leaders reverted to squabbling, and north and south combined against Cyfeiliog—who had extended his control over Rhuddlan and Prestatyn in the north and Brecon and lower Cardiganshire in the south. The lords of the north and south took back Rhuddlan and Prestatyn, and once more split Wales deeper than ever into opposing factions. Wales never again came so close to achieving one united independent state.

# R

**Raglan Castle,** *Raglan, Monmouthshire. 9½ miles north-east of Pontypool off A40.*

The famed magnificence of Raglan Castle's structure most probably dated from foundations laid in 1430, though building went on for 40 years. However, some say it dates from the days of Henry VII (1485–1509), others that a Sir John Morley was Lord of Raglan Castle in 1377. Another source says it was begun by Sir William Thomas, who fought with Henry V at Agincourt in 1415, and was knighted on the battlefield as he lay dying from his wounds. Yet another source says there was a fortification on the site in the mid-12th Century, during Henry II's reign. This is quite likely, since the castle is on a motte and bailey site and it is also most likely that 1430 saw the start on the new hold. The Wars of the Roses marked the end of the medieval systems in England, and nothing like Raglan would have been built after that date. But it is likely that Raglan was the last great castle to be built, and that it marks the end of the Middle Ages, as clearly as did the Wars of the Roses themselves. It was probably built with the Wars in mind, being attributed to William Herbert, Earl of Pembroke, an ardent Yorkist.

Ancient writers were, however, unanimous on its quality, one describing it as "the most perfect decorated stronghold of which this country can boast". The castle covers over four acres, and was dominated by the mighty hexagonal keep, Melin y Gwent (Yellow Tower of Gwent). This was surrounded by its own chemise wall, had walls ten feet thick, and with its five storeys was possibly the tallest tower in England and Wales. A fine twin-towered gatehouse led into the large outer ward, and when this was built the earlier small gatehouse was walled up. The castle was further defended by three large, and two small, polygonal towers.

In the Wars of the Roses the Earl of Pembroke was captured by Lancastrian forces, and beheaded in 1469. Sixteen years later Henry VII (who had once been imprisoned in Raglan Castle) came to the throne and ended the long and bitter rift. Raglan then had to wait until Charles I's reign before becoming prominent once more. By then it was a splendid castle with magnificent halls—one of them measuring 66 feet by 28 feet, with a rare geometrical roof laid with Irish oak, and lit from a large cupola. The Earl was also an accomplished engineer and inventor, and the many water displays were an impressive feature at the castle, one fountain spouting a column as high as the castle walls. Raglan was frequently visited by Charles I, and after the Civil War broke out in 1642 Raglan set the pattern for the rest of Monmouthshire by immediately declaring for the Royalist cause. After the defeat at Naseby Charles stayed again at Raglan, which had not only been defending itself, but also engaging in frequent battles with the Parliamentarians who had captured Monmouth Castle.

Raglan's was the last garrison in the south to surrender to the Parliamentarians in 1646, after a long siege mounted by Sir Thomas Fairfax with 3,500 soldiers. The castle was then largely dismantled, its lead and timber being taken to Monmouth and thence by boat to Bristol where a bridge was being rebuilt. The great tower presented unusual problems, however; Cromwell's men eventually undermined the tower, then burnt the props to collapse it, and the tower sank to the position in which it may be seen today. After the Restoration of 1660 Charles II piled honours on the family, and the 2nd Marquess, as he had then become, continued his experiments with steam and water; he wrote a paper describing an engine—which was eventually developed into the first steam driven pump. Not surprisingly, his inventions led to numerous stories. One unsubstantiated account is of the Earl's garrison beating back the attacking Parliamentarians with jets of water from hoses. Another, equally unsubstantiated, claims that when a group of Parliamentarians was in the castle searching for arms (no date was given for this event)

*Raglan Castle, one of the last true medieval castles to be built in Britain, was the home of the Earls of Pembroke. It was slighted by Cromwell's soldiers after the Civil War*

*Rhuddlan Castle, a monument to the iron will of Edward I. It was here that he enforced harsh peace terms on Llywelyn in 1277. Earlier fortifications on the site were captured by Harold Godwinsson three years before his death at the Battle of Hastings*

the Earl started up some of his engines, water displays and experiments, and the sudden noise and spectacle sent the intruders fleeing.

**Rhuddlan Castle,** *Rhuddlan, Flintshire. 3 miles south of Rhyl off A525.*

Fortifications of some sort at Rhuddlan can be traced all the way back to the 8th Century, for its position at the lowest crossable point on the Clwyd has given it a strategic importance that involved it in the struggles of Wales against England on and off for 600 years. The first known conquest of Rhuddlan was in A.D. 796 when English forces crossed Offa's Dyke and won control over a large district of which Rhuddlan was the centre; but the absence of English place-names in the area seems to indicate that their settlement could not have lasted long. Rhuddlan soon became the seat of the princes of North Wales. Eventually it became the stronghold of Gruffydd ap Llywelyn, who carried out many raids into England as far as Oswestry and Wrexham until in 1063 Harold Godwinsson, "Last of the Saxons", took Rhuddlan and destroyed Gruffydd's stronghold.

Three years later came the Norman invasion and the death of Harold, heralding a conquest of Wales far more thorough than any experienced since the Romans. By 1073 a typical Norman motte and bailey castle rose over the ruins of the old Welsh fort. This castle, founded by Robert of Rhuddlan, deputy of the Earl of Chester, used a most substantial motte which is still an impressive sight (the mound is called Twthill) south of the present castle, and the shape of the bailey can also be made out.

Rhuddlan became a notable stronghold as Robert extended widespread control, while a township, with a mint as well as a church, grew under the protection of the castle. Nevertheless Rhuddlan was still in a strategically important position and the wooden fortification changed hands in a number of border skirmishes. There is no indication or past record of what this castle looked like, but it is unlikely that it had any stone structure. Certainly all the buildings in the bailey, such as the chapel, were wood, though it is possible that some of the defences had been strengthened with stone.

Eventually Llywelyn ap Gruffydd, Prince of Wales, united all the princes of the north under him, and while Henry III was tied down by the baronial unrest in England Llywelyn began to enlist baronial support in Wales. He achieved recognition and many concessions from Henry, and won Simon de Montfort as a powerful ally. But Llywelyn also tried to defy the new king, Edward I, an act which marked the beginning of the end for the Prince, and the beginning of a new era for Rhuddlan. In the summer of 1277 Edward moved his large army and all its supplies into Wales from Chester to Flint and a month later, having begun the building of Flint Castle, he moved to Rhuddlan. In October Llywelyn surrendered, and a month later submitted to Edward's uncompromising peace terms before the king at Rhuddlan.

Edward began the castle at Rhuddlan as soon as he arrived, for payments for work done on the site were first recorded on 14th September 1277. Work progressed quickly, and by spring 1282 a great deal had been achieved. In charge of the building's design and construction was James of St. George, who was also supervising Flint Castle and later, as Master of the King's Works, was to build the castles at Caernarvon, Conway and Harlech. The main defences were completed in 1282, which was fortunate, for in that year Llywelyn's brother Dafydd sparked off another Welsh rising, with the Prince's immediate support. The Welsh attacked Rhuddlan, but in vain, and before the year was out Llywelyn was dead and Dafydd was captured. To Rhuddlan came Dafydd, on his way to execution at Shrewsbury; and to Rhuddlan also came Llywelyn's head, cut from his body after his almost accidental death (see Aberedw Castle), on its way to be exhibited outside the Tower of London.

The castle that James of St. George built was—and still is—a substantial one, though it is no longer obviously concentric, for most of the outer curtain has disappeared. One unusual feature of its design was the placing of the two double-towered gatehouses on two of the angles of the square inner ward. The other two angles have single round towers of the identical size and shape to the ones used in the gatehouses—so the quadrilateral inner curtain has six towers. The outer ward is fairly wide and slopes quite steeply down to the Clwyd on the south-west. It was ringed by a moat (except where it fronted the river) which was partly flooded by the tidal flow of the Clwyd, and had revetted sides. The outer curtain was polygonal with numerous turrets, four gates, and a substantial tower—Gillot's Tower—which guarded the south apex on the river where ships could shelter. This tower can still be seen in a reasonably complete state. Traces of old turning bridge arrangements can be seen in two of the gates. Except for traces of foundations in the north-west corner nothing remains of the numerous buildings which once rose in the outer bailey, such as the granary, stables, and blacksmith's forge; or of the various artillery pieces or "engines" which would have stood there.

The inner ward, the castle proper, is still in comparatively good condition, however, and all four sections of the inner curtain are still intact to the height of the wall walk, though the battlements have gone except for one small length. Also vanished are the small turrets which made a type of machicolation in the centre of each side, though their position can easily be seen on two of the walls. Some of the towers are also still at their original height (though again without battlements), and the remarkable—and unusual—symmetry of the building is immediately apparent. The domestic buildings that once occupied the inner ward have left no trace, though a 50-foot deep well remains near the centre.

The town was also defended, although, as in the case of Flint, these defences were of earthworks and timber only. The town defences belong to the period 1280–82, and after that most of the domestic buildings in the castle were completed. A massive project was also undertaken to further Edward's combination of sea and land power. This involved turning the sluggish, meandering Clwyd estuary into a straight, sufficiently deep canal two miles long which gave Rhuddlan access to the sea. Digging the canal was, for those days, a massive task, and it took an average of over seventy men three years to complete. The total cost of the fortification at Rhuddlan—castle, canal and town—amounted in today's terms to at least £1½ million.

As the king's headquarters during both Welsh campaigns (the great castles at Caernarvon, Conway, and Harlech were only begun after Llywelyn's death, and Beaumaris was started years later), Rhuddlan saw a great deal of Edward I, and there is some conjecture that the traditional presentation of his infant son, in accordance with his promise to give the Welsh people a future king, born in Wales, who could speak no English, and whose life was blameless, took place at Rhuddlan Castle and not at Caernarvon (see Caernarvon Castle). This argument holds that Edward had made the promise at Rhuddlan, and that he was at Rhuddlan in 1284 when he heard of his son's birth at Caernarvon. It was then that he named him Edward and announced the birth. It is possible that Edward was at Rhuddlan when the birth took place, though he did soon travel to Caernarvon. It is also true that when he was four months old the young Edward was brought to Rhuddlan Castle, and that within those four months his brother Alfonso had died, making Edward heir to the throne. So it is quite likely that at least a similar presentation took place at Rhuddlan. (Seventeen years after his birth, the Prince of Wales returned to Rhuddlan on a tour of his principality, receiving the homage of his subjects.) Also in 1284 Edward I proclaimed the new administrative and judicial structure of Wales, creating the present shires of Anglesey, Caernarvon, Cardigan, Carmarthen, Flint and Merioneth, which was to remain largely unchanged until Henry VIII's Act of Union in 1536.

Rhuddlan escaped the uprising of 1294 in which Caernarvon Castle was captured and most of Edward's castles were isolated, but the township was ravaged during Owain Glyndwr's revolt at the beginning of the 15th Century. Except for that episode it was a peaceful centre of administrative and judicial control for much of Wales, until the Civil War. Then it was garrisoned for Charles I, but four years later, in 1646, surrendered to Major-General Mytton and his Parliamentary forces. The

Royalist stronghold was wrecked by order of Parliament in May 1648, and four years later a poet described it as a "wind and war-shaken castle". Thereafter it continued to decay steadily—especially when it was used as a ready-made quarry—until guardianship passed to the Government in 1944 and restoration was begun.

and became the mistress of Charles II. Their son was acknowledged by Charles, who made him Duke of Monmouth—the doomed leader of the rebellion against James II.

The castle was greatly neglected after the Civil War, but in 1900 Viscount St. David began extensive restoration, and subsequent owners have continued this. It is therefore considerably altered, but the tower is unmistakable for miles around, and traces of the old earthwork bailey can be seen at the foot of the outcrop.

**Roch Castle,** *Roch, Pembrokeshire. 6 miles north-east of Haverfordwest off A487.*

This castle was founded in the second half of the 13th Century, although the lordship de Rupe (rock) can be traced back to about 1200. An earlier fortress may have existed here, but the prominent D-shaped tower on this isolated rocky outcrop is thought to have been built by Adam de Rupe. The family had played an important role in the English settlement of Pembrokeshire, and owned considerable territory in the northern areas. Roch Castle was doubtless built as one of the outer defences of "Little England" or "Landsker", for it is near the unmarked border which for centuries has separated the English and Welsh areas of Pembrokeshire. A legend is told of the castle's founder, Adam de Rupe, whose fear of a prophecy that he would be killed by a viper's bite led him to choose the isolated site. Apparently he was unable to avoid his fate, for a viper, concealed in a bundle of firewood, found its way into the castle and fulfilled the prophecy.

The de Rupe, or Roche, family came to an end in 1420 and the castle changed ownership a number of times until it came into the possession of the Walter family, who owned it when the Civil War broke out in 1642. Although Walter saw out the war in the safety of London his castle was garrisoned by the Royalists, and was involved in much action in 1644 when it was taken by the Parliamentarians, recaptured by the Royalists, and then fell once again to Cromwell's forces. Walter did not return to Roch Castle, going instead to the Hague, but his daughter Lucy stayed in London

**Rug Castell,** *Corwen, Merioneth. 10 miles south-south-west of Ruthin.*

This area is quite liberally scattered with the sites of old motte and bailey castles, ring works, moats, forts, and camps, so a documentary mention of 1160 may not refer to this particular site.

**Rumney Castle,** *Rumney, Monmouthshire. 3 miles north-east of Cardiff on A48.*

Only a low motte remains, and a mention in the Pipe Roll of 1184 to a "castellum Remmi" provides the only possible link with its past.

**Ruthin Castle,** *Ruthin, Denbighshire. Southern part of town on A494.*

Ruthin Castle was a strong baronial castle ordered by Edward I, probably in 1277, though it seems that most work took place in 1282. It had two wards, the outer one being smaller than the inner. Five round towers originally guarded the inner ward, but only the remains of three of them are left, together with the ruined double-towered gatehouse.

The Lordship Marcher of Dyffryn Clwyd was given to the Grey family in 1282 after Llewelyn's defeat and the end of the principality of North Wales, and the history of the castle until 1400 seems to have been uneventful. When the 15th Century began the castle was held by Lord Grey, who had previously

attempted to acquire, by devious means, the Dee estates of a Welshman named Owain Glyndwr. For a number of years animosity had built up between them, and when Glyndwr was ready to launch his bid for an independent Wales, Ruthin and Lord Grey presented a satisfying target for the first blow. Glyndwr's attack surprised all England and Wales, but nowhere more so than Ruthin, and the town was ravaged and burnt. Ruthin Castle, however, managed to hold out, but the Welsh rebel was not to be done out of his vengeance. Two years later he defeated an English force at Vyrnwy, captured Lord Grey and imprisoned him in Dolbadarn Castle—eventually releasing him on payment of a ransom of 10,000 marks.

In the Civil War Ruthin Castle resisted an attack by Parliamentary forces, who returned to besiege it two years later in 1646. The Royalist garrison surrendered to Major-General Mytton, and the castle was destroyed by order of Parliament. Part of the ruins were incorporated in a large castellated mansion which took the name of the castle, and this was at one time the seat of Colonel Cornwallis West, a descendant of Sir Thomas Myddelton who

*Ruthin; the original castle was the scene of a violent feud between the Welsh patriot Owain Glyndwr and the Marcher Lord, Lord Grey*

was Lord Mayor of London in 1613, and who subsidised the publication of the first popular Welsh Bible.

*S*

**St. Donat's Castle,** *Llantwit Major, Glamorgan. On coast $7\frac{1}{2}$ miles south of Bridgend.*

The early history of this castle in its striking setting is unknown, though tradition holds that its founder was Guillaume le Esterling, the ancestor of the Stradling family. It has been constantly occupied since it was built in the late 13th or early 14th Century, but frequent additions and alterations have changed it considerably. There may have been an earlier earthwork there, for the site is a rounded shape. The castle had a concentric plan, a polygonal outer ward enclosing an angular inner ward defended by several towers, but the later alterations turned it into a baronial hall rather than a military stronghold.

**St. Fagan's Castle,** *St. Fagans, Glamorgan. 4 miles west of Cardiff.*

The early history of this site is unknown and little can be traced, for the 16th Century Tudor mansion with its many gables has almost entirely obscured the early remains. Some of the old curtain wall can still be seen; this is thought to date from the 13th Century, and the remains of a keep may be hidden among the newer structure. Close to the mansion is the site of one of the bloodiest battles of the Civil War, in which the New Model Army of the Parliamentarians, under Colonel Horton, crushed the Royalist resurgents in the brief second Civil War of 1648.

The Windsor family held St. Fagan's Castle from 1730, and it was eventually presented to the National Museum of Wales by the Earl of Plymouth, to be used as the Welsh National Folk Museum. The castle itself, with its gardens, is a principal feature of the museum, which in its 98 acre park also has numerous reconstructed buildings from many parts of Wales, representing dates back to the 14th century.

**St. Quintin's Castle**—*see Llanblethian Castle.*

**Sennybridge Castle**—*see Castell Du.*

**Sentence Castle,** *Templeton, Pembrokeshire. 2 miles south of Narberth.*

Sentence Castle, at Nat. Grid Ref. SN 110116, was the predecessor of Narberth Castle, at SN 109144. It used to be called Narberth Castle, and dates from the end of the 11th Century. It was destroyed in 1116, and again in 1215, but nothing is known of its founder, and it was not mentioned in the records after its capture by the Welsh in 1220.

**Skenfrith Castle,** *Skenfrith, Monmouthshire. $5\frac{1}{2}$ miles north-north-west of Monmouth on B4521.*

The three castles of Grosmont, Skenfrith, and White formed the Norman defences on the Welsh borderland of Gwent, and Skenfrith was originally built as a motte and bailey castle in the early 12th Century. The remains which can now be seen, however, date from the early 13th Century, and the round keep on the motte is the principal feature. This was surrounded by a four-sided curtain wall, probably with five towers, though the remains of only four are left. Skenfrith Castle was always closely connected with its companion strongholds Grosmont Castle and White Castle, and accounts of those castles should be read to trace its history. In 1936 it was given to the National Trust, and guardianship has been entrusted to the Department of the Environment.

**Swansea Castle,** *Swansea, Glamorgan. Part of new buildings in centre of town.*

The Normans spread quickly into South Wales; in 1099 Henry Beaumont captured Gower, and he was the founder of Swansea Castle. That first castle, however, has vanished completely, and the remains which are now incorporated into an office building date from the early 14th Century fortified manor house built by Henry Gower, Bishop of St. David's. This building consisted of a range of buildings joining a small round turret to a large

*The keep at Skenfrith, which with Grosmont and White Castles guarded the borderland of Gwent for the Normans*

quadrilateral tower. The old castle was frequently attacked, captured and recaptured, and the Bishop's fortress suffered greatly at the hands of Owain Glyndwr at the beginning of the 15th Century.

# T

**Tenby Castle,** *Tenby, Pembrokeshire. On sea front of town.*

The Welsh stronghold at Tenby was captured by the Normans at the beginning of the 12th Century, and became part of the heavily settled area where the Welsh language was seldom heard. An early keep was constructed, its capture in 1152 being recorded, and there is now a small museum in the keep. The site gave the castle great strength, increased by a D-shaped barbican in the early 13th Century, and a small watch tower, probably many years later. Much of the castle's strength, however, came from the town defences, a masonry wall already encircling the town in the 13th Century. The walls were strengthened in 1457 and further in 1588, and the five-arched main gate is extremely impressive.

In the Civil War which began in 1642 Tenby twice suffered bombardment from the sea, and fell to the Parliamentarians in 1644. Tenby was also involved in the revolt of 1648 when so many Parliamentarians joined the Royalists cause and began the second Civil War, but it fell once more to Cromwell's forces.

**Tomen Castell,** *Dolwyddelan, Caernarvonshire. 5 miles south-west of Betwys-y-Coed on A496.*

There are traces of a rectangular tower on the rocky site of this old Welsh castle, which may be the castle behind the tradition of a 12th Century castle which preceded the present Dolwyddelan Castle. Tomen Castell is at Nat. Grid Ref. SH 724521, and Dolwyddelan Castle at SH 722523.

**Tomen Castle,** *Llanfihangel nant Melan, Radnorshire. 7 miles east of Llandrindod Wells on A44.*

An old stronghold, a mound fortified by earthworks, without recorded history or traceable original form.

**Towy Castle,** *Llandyfaelog, Carmarthenshire. 3½ miles south of Carmarthen off A484.*

For hundreds of years Towy Castle has simply been the name of a field, but recently ploughing turned up the rubble of a mortared building, and

*Swansea Castle, the remains of a fortress of the Bishops of St. David's in the 14th Century*

some pieces of green glazed pottery. As yet, no excavations have been carried out.

**Tretower Castle,** *Tretower, Breconshire. $1\frac{1}{2}$ miles north-west of Crickhowell off A479.*

The first stronghold raised at Tretower was a motte which apparently had the unusual feature of being revetted in stone as it was built (this was normally an extra defensive step which could be added later). The revettment continued above the motte to form a polygonal shell. The date of this early and seemingly strong defence is unknown, but it was founded by a Norman knight called Picard, and it is known that the Picards were in the district by 1106.

The small castle was captured by the Welsh in 1233, but reverted to the English when the uprising was crushed. It was probably then that the bailey was added; there is no sign of it having any earthworks, but a stone wall with three round towers, two of which enclose the gate—a structure that would not have been attempted for a castle of this type before about the mid-13th Century. At the same time a tall round keep was built in the middle of the polygonal shell on the motte. Unfortunately most of the castle has been ruined.

Tretower Castle, reinforced as it was, once again succumbed to a Welsh uprising in 1322, though again for a limited time. Tretower Castle was listed in 1403 as a defensible stronghold for Henry IV, and it had its chance to justify the claim when Sir James Berkeley successfully withstood an attack by Owain Glyndwr a year later. Soon afterwards it passed into the possession of Sir Roger Vaughan. The castle's residential potential had been increased by the addition of a manor house in the 14th Century, but the Vaughans rebuilt this, making one of the finest examples of a fortified manor house in Wales. It replaced the castle as the lord's residence, and Tretower Court is now as great an attraction as the castle ruins.

**Usk Castle,** *Usk, Monmouthshire. In town 6 miles east of Pontypool, off A499.*

The ruins of Usk Castle reflect well the proportions of the original, although they date back to at least four different phases of building. The earliest part is the earthwork of the inner ward, which contains the small square keep. This was the castle that was founded in the late 12th Century by the de Clare family as a Marcher Lord stronghold. The castle was captured by Welsh rebels in 1233 and again in 1265, and during that part of the 13th Century the outer ward was built; the gatehouse dates from this period. The impressive round tower was probably added in the late 13th Century, and further buildings in the outer ward were put up in the 15th Century. Usk Castle was listed as defensible in the 1403 records, but the tradition that it surrendered to Owain Glyndwr's forces soon thereafter is not well founded. The castle was a Royalist hold in the Civil War, and was subsequently destroyed by the Parliamentarians.

**Welshpool Castell,** *Welshpool, Montgomeryshire. On east side of town.*

This is the site of a motte and bailey castle which was captured by mining in 1196, but recaptured shortly after by its Welsh builders. It was one of the predecessors of Powis Castle.

**Weobley Castle,** *Llanrhidian, Glamorgan. 11½ miles west of Swansea.*

The first documentary evidence of building at Weobly is found in a listing of the knight tenants of William de Braose, Lord of Gower, but it is not until 1397 that mention can be found of owners' names. However, it is believed that the sub-lordship of Weobley was first held by the de la Bere family when it was set up after the Norman conquest of Gower early in the 12th Century. The castle site was probably a later addition to the lordship, while the castle itself was begun at the end of the 13th Century and completed early in the next, although additions to the castle continued during the following two centuries.

There is some indication that the castle was meant to be bigger than it eventually was. It is formed by a number of buildings adjoining to enclose a courtyard, their outer walls forming the outside of the castle; so that except for the short wall and the gateway on the west side, Weobley has no such thing as a curtain wall. Strictly, Weobley Castle is not so much a castle as a fortified manor house, and its present well-preserved remains provide interesting evidence of domestic arrangements at the end of the Middle Ages. The important rooms were all on the first floor—the solar over the cellar (which was really a ground floor chamber, but unlit), the hall adjacent to the solar and above the kitchen, a guest chamber, and a chapel.

Even as a fortified manor, Weobley was not particularly strong. The square south-west tower, and the adjoining wall section towards the gate and the cellar corner, were never completed above the top of the ground floor level, and eventually this part was abandoned altogether. The tower, (with the hall block across the courtyard the earliest structures), is now rather badly ruined and the rooms on the east side are also incomplete.

Weobley Castle escaped conflict until Owain

*The peaceful setting of Tretower Castle, a stronghold built by a Norman named Picard at the turn of the 11th Century*

Glyndwr's revolt. The stronghold was attacked and doubtless damaged, but by 1406 the old order was returning. Although a report of 1410 described the castle as having been destroyed by the Welsh, it is likely that the state of the unfinished tower gave the castle a worse appearance than it deserved, and the castle was soon re-occupied. Later in the 15th Century Weobley passed into the possession of Sir Rhys ap Thomas, Henry VII's ardent and loyal supporter; but when Henry VIII had Sir Rhys's grandson and heir Rhys ap Gruffydd executed for treason the estates passed to the Crown and were sold to Sir William Herbert, Earl of Pembroke. Occupancy was given to tenants, and part of it (the 15th Century porch rooms which adjoined the hall) were altered by a farmer to make his residence in the 16th Century. The rest of the castle gradually decayed; in 1666 it was sold to Sir Edward Mansel, and from the Mansels it passed to the Talbots, who placed it under the guardianship of the Government in 1911. The hall is the main feature of the ruins, but the whole still forms an interesting, compact monument to the Middle Ages.

**White Castle,** *Llantilio Crossenny, Monmouthshire. 5½ miles east-north-east of Abergavenny between B4233 and B4521.*

White Castle, or The White Castle, is one of the best preserved fortresses of the Marches, and in much better condition than the castles of Grosmont or Skenfrith, with which it formed a defensive line against the Welsh of Gwent. It is also interesting as one of the best examples of a ring castle. The 12th Century castle was at first a low inner ward and a small crescent-shaped bailey, both of which were well defended by strong earthworks, the inner ward being completely encircled by a substantial moat. This ward has a small square keep, but the bailey had no masonry walls. The inner ward was walled with short straight lengths curving up from the

keep, giving it the shape of an egg, with the keep forming the entrance to the enclosure at the "blunt" end. In the middle or late 13th Century most of the keep was demolished and six round towers put up at intervals around the curtain, the sharp end of the "egg" being replaced by the gate formed by two of the round towers. Across the moat from the gateway, and at the opposite end of the site from the early bailey, a new, large bailey was made, again well ditched, and walled with a gate, three round towers, and a rectangular tower. The likely date for the construction of the early work—the remains of the keep are the oldest part of the ruins—has been deduced as between 1138 and 1155. It was then known as Llantilio Castle, and Llantilio was mentioned in a charter of 1137 in which King Stephen granted the holdings of Payn FitzJohn to his son-in-law, Roger of Gloucester. But the charter, while mentioning Skenfrith, Grosmont and Llantilio, does not specifically mention a castle at the latter site; if one existed it was probably a small timber fort, and not necessarily on exactly the same spot as the later castle. There do not appear to be any other documents relevant to that area until the royal accounts (the Pipe Roll) of Henry II which start in 1155. They would have recorded the expenses of Llantilio Castle, but there is no entry until 1161, when £19 17s 4d is charged to payments to knights and for repairs to the castles of Llantilion, Skenfrith and Grosmont. Between 1184 and 1186 the equivalent of about £18,000 was spent at Skenfrith, and this was doubtless for the curtain wall which enclosed the inner ward.

In 1201 White (Llantilio), Grosmont and Skenfrith were granted by King John to Hubert de Burgh, and in 1205 they were transferred to William de Braose, who lost his estates when he fell from royal favour. During the baronial revolt at the end of King John's reign de Braose's son recovered the castles, but by 1219 Hubert de Burgh had risen to Justiciar and Earl of Kent, and the King's Court, then the highest court in the country, had no hesitation in restoring the three castles to him. Hubert de Burgh fell from favour in 1232, and custody was granted to a Peter des Rivaux, the nephew of the Bishop of Winchester. His career came to an end two years later, and the castles went to the Crown. They were put under the charge of the German Waleran for a number of years, and much of the

*White Castle, held at various times in the 13th Century by the powerful families of de Burgh and de Braose. It is one of the best preserved of the Marcher castles*

13th Century building was done in 1244. Perhaps the covering of the castle in the light plaster which gave it its new name dates from this time—though now only fragments of this plaster remain. It was subsequently given to Prince Edward, who became Edward I, and he gave the castle—and its two companions—to his brother Edmund "Crouchback", Earl of Lancaster. Edward also spent a considerable amount on defence, for by then the Welsh under Llywelyn, Prince of Wales, were growing steadily more threatening; if Abergavenny Castle were to fall White Castle would have formed the front line of defence. As king, Edward removed that threat in 1277, and destroyed it forever in 1282, and White Castle lost its military importance. By the 16th Century it was derelict. In 1825 it was sold to the Duke of Beaufort, and in 1922 the Government were appointed guardians by its owner, Sir Henry Mather Jackson.

**Wiston Castle,** *Wiston, Pembrokeshire. 4½ miles east-north-east of Haverfordwest.*

Wiston Castle was also called Castell Gwis, and was a predecessor of Picton Castle. It was a low motte and bailey castle with a polygonal shell-wall on the motte made of rubble. The doorway still shows the socket for the draw bar, and the structure of the castle can be followed. The bailey seems never to have been walled, and the shell of the motte probably dates from the late 12th Century. "Castellum Wiz" was mentioned as being captured in 1147, although the man who probably founded it, Wizo, died in 1130. After it was captured once more in 1220 there were apparently plans to rebuild it, but Wiston Castle does not figure in the records again.

**Wolf's Castle,** *Wolf's Castle, Pembrokeshire. 7 miles north of Haverfordwest on A40.*

Although it has given its name to the village as well, there seems to be no recorded history of this site. Not far away is Trefgarn, claimed to be the birthplace of Owain Glyndwr, whose rebellion at the beginning of the 15th Century so disrupted Wales.

**Ystradmeurig Castle,** *Ystradmeurig, Cardiganshire. 12 miles south-east of Aberystwyth on B4340.*

The castle at Ystradmeurig now displays only a few mounds and traces of the foundations of a square tower. There was a motte castle only slightly further east, at Nat. Grid Ref. SN 717677, and it is possible that Ystradmeurig at SN 702675 replaced this. One of the sites was mentioned in records of 1116, and was destroyed in 1137. In 1151 the castle of Ystradmeurig was rebuilt and then destroyed in 1208, and these entries probably relate to both sites. 1151, therefore, is the likely date when the present Ystradmeurig Castle—such as it is—was built, and there was no further mention of the place after 1208.

# Y

*Weobley, strictly speaking a fortified manor rather than a castle*